fee

worcestershire
c o u n t y c o u n c i l
Libraries & Learning

feeding kids

the
netmums
cookery book

with Judith Wills

headline

 netmums

Netmums is the largest parenting organisation in the UK with 500,000 members, all mums, sharing information, making friends and offering each other advice and support on a wealth of subjects relating to parenting, children and life in general. Feeding kids is always a hot topic and so many great recipes, tips and ideas have been shared by our members that they just had to be put in a book. So here it is!

To become a member of Netmums (a free service) – for up-to-date food news and advice on feeding the family; or for local and national support in parenting – go to **www.netmums.com**.

Siobhan Freegard

I left Ireland for the bright lights of London at the age of eighteen, where I got an office job and worked my way up the corporate ladder. I married Paul, an Englishman, and we had our first child in 1996. Having a baby turned my priorities on their heads. I went back to work, but within two years I realised I wanted to spend more time at home and I took a year off from my career. I now have three children, Sean, Aisling and Aran and ten years later I am still on 'my year off'! Netmums came about from my own experiences of being a new mum – pretty much the same experiences as all new mums, but I thought it would be useful to share them, to show you that you are not on your own.

Cathy Court

I studied Physiology and Biochemistry at Reading University, and have always been interested in food and nutrition. My interest in the importance of what we eat was magnified when I had my children, Alfie and Amelia, and saw the bad effect E-numbers, junk food and highly processed foods had on them. I helped set up Netmums in the early days and am now privileged to combine my two passions, Netmums and nutrition, by writing and editing the Netmums food section.

Judith Wills

I am a mum myself, and known for offering sensible and practical advice to families on healthy eating and weight control, but I also love cooking and eating good food. I am viewed as one of the UK's leading nutrition experts and have sold over 2 million books worldwide.

For advice on all food- and health-related issues and problems, or to email Judith Wills, go to www.thedietdetective.net.

By Netmums and available from Headline

Feeding Kids: The Netmums Cookery Book, with Judith Wills

How to Be a Happy Mum: The Netmums Guide to Stress-free Family Life, with Siobhan Freegard

Toddling to Ten: Your Common Parenting Problems Solved, with Hollie Smith

Your Pregnancy: The Netmums Guide to Having A Baby, with Hilary Pereira

Baby's First Year: The Netmums Guide to Being A New Mum, with Hollie Smith

Other titles in the netmums series

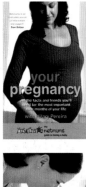

First published in 2007

by HEADLINE PUBLISHING GROUP

First published in trade paperback in 2009

by HEADLINE PUBLISHING GROUP

1

Cataloguing in Publication Data is available from the British Library

Trade paperback 978 0 7553 1605 2

Typeset in Arial Rounded and Conduit

Printed and bound in Great Britain by Butler Tanner and Dennis Ltd, Frome, Somerset

Editor: Susan Fleming

Photographs: Robin Matthews

Design: www.timpattinson.com

Headline's policy is to use papers that are natural, renewable and recyclable products and made from wood grown in sustainable forests. The logging and manufacturing processes are expected to conform to the environmental regulations of the country of origin.

HEADLINE PUBLISHING GROUP
An Hachette Livre UK Company
338 Euston Road
London NW1 3BH

www.headline.co.uk
www.netmums.com
www.hachettelivre.co.uk

CONTENTS

Acknowledgments

SF and CC: First and foremost we'd like to thank all the Netmums members who contributed their favourite recipes. Their ideas and suggestions are what makes this book. To the best of our knowledge, unless otherwise acknowledged, these are home-grown recipes and have been adapted for our purposes.

Thanks to our gorgeous photo-shoot models for being so patient: Harry Brew, Cleo Coleman, Alfie Court, Amelia Court, Finlay Eaton, Jayden Griffin, Ben Jenks, Oliver Jenks, Samuel Jenks, Henriette McArdell, Max Noble, Joseph O'Neill, Alex O'Neill, Isabelle O' Neill, Lily O'Neill, Angelica Papapavlou, Mariella Papapavlou, Charlotte Russell, James Russell and Kiri Simpson.

Thanks to Imani Cracknell for the delightful drawings.

Thanks to Lorraine Jenks for preparing and presenting the meals for the photo-shoot; your calmness was inspirational.

Thanks to all the Netmums team for their help testing the recipes, and their children for tasting the results. Special thanks to Lisa Marsden, whom we kept very busy in the kitchen for several weeks.

Thanks to our agent Jane Turnbull who made the idea for this book become a reality, and Andrea Henry and the team from Headline for believing in 'a bunch of mums'.

JW: I would like to thank everyone at Headline (especially Andrea Henry and Susan Fleming); Siobhan Freegard and Cathy Court for being such enthusiastic and efficient working partners; Jane Turnbull for introducing me to the truly ground-breaking organisation Netmums; and all the Netmums members who sent in their recipes and tips for this unique book.

Advice on how to cut back on salt, sugar and fats is by Judith Wills, based on information from the Food Standards Agency.

Introduction

Why is it that just because you become a mum (or a dad), you are expected automatically to know how to cook healthy, nutritious and delicious meals? And not only should you know how to do it, you should do it cheerfully and enthusiastically three times a day, seven days a week. And that's as well as looking after the children, being up half the night with babies, keeping the house from resembling a bombsite, getting to the supermarket, being a washerwoman, ironing lady, gardener and odd-job-mum and probably holding down a job as well. Wonderful parents that we are, we somehow manage to put food on the table every day.

Good food is necessary for our children's mental and physical health – both now and in the future. Food is also emotionally important: family meals mean time spent together, food enjoyed together and friends invited to eat with us. It's the stuff childhood memories are made of.

Home cooking is important in so many ways and yet, for so many reasons, it can be the thing that slips close to the bottom of our long list of daily chores. But does cooking have to be such a chore? It shouldn't be and doesn't need to be. A little knowledge, a few ideas and bit of planning can make all the difference.

The 100-plus recipes in this book, plus ideas for infinite variations, will help you to put appetising and healthy meals on the table every day, 365 days a year. They will help you to help your child enjoy good food. By that, we mean food that is of good quality, tastes good and does him or her good, too.

This book will help you to understand what a healthy diet for kids is, and how to provide it without too much hassle. We also help you to understand food labels so that you can buy commercial products that fit happily into a balanced diet for the family. We've offered you some help as well with planning the family meals, as a little planning really does go a long way. Each recipe is health rated using traffic light symbols for salt, fat, saturated fat and sugar levels and includes Nutrition Notes to give you some pointers on the health benefits.

And because all children are different, there will always be a vast difference between the rosy picture of you putting food on the table and them eating up every last crumb with delight, and what really happens. The fussy eaters, the food refusal, the kids with no appetite, the veggie haters and the fads and even fears that many children go through, means that their relationship with food – and your relationship with them in the kitchen – is not always easy. And so we also look at some of the most common problems you are likely to encounter and help you to deal with them.

Feeding kids – A survival guide

Often the advertisers' cosy portrayal of family mealtimes is a world apart from the reality – and sometimes feeding the kids really does seem like the hardest kind of SAS course. All your parenting skills are needed to survive *their* fads, fusses, fancies and refusals. And, let's face it, mealtimes often mean hours of *your* time.

At Netmums we hear daily about all of our members' worries about feeding their kids. Judith, our Diet Detective, gets dozens of letters a week from mums battling with all kinds of feeding problems when all they want to do is simply give their children a healthy and enjoyable diet.

So in this chapter we discuss the problems that are the most common, in our experience, and offer our top tips on practical ways to make mealtimes both peaceful and nutritious.

Top 5 Netmums Tips

Make time for food! We all lead super-busy lives, but because food is such an important part of our children's health and wellbeing, it is vital to add 'good food for the family' to the list of things that are important to you. That doesn't mean you have to spend hours slaving in the kitchen. But the food providers in the family need to have respect for food and for eating and to make time for its preparation and eating together whenever possible. Most of the recipes in this book are not time consuming and will provide inspiration.

Lead by example. Don't buy what you don't want them to eat. Get your children interested in what they eat; in how and where it is bought, how it is prepared and cooked. Most small children love helping with food and when they're young you can nurture in them a real love of good ingredients, natural tastes and new things.

Help your children understand why good food is important for their healthy bodies. If there is a lull in the conversation at mealtimes you could sometimes play a 'Do you know?' game. For example, 'Do you know why cheese is good for you?' (Because it contains calcium for strong bones and protein for building healthy muscles.) 'Do you know why carrots are orange?' (Because they contain lots of carotene, which helps give you good eyesight and healthy skin.) The nutrition notes on the recipes in this book will provide plenty of information so that you can play the game with confidence.

Help them maintain a reasonable weight by watching portion sizes, letting them get plenty of fresh air and exercise between meals, and avoiding too many foods, snacks and drinks that are high in fat and sugar.

Make mealtimes enjoyable and relaxed. Children will learn to associate good healthy food with pleasure.

Top 10 Netmums Questions and Answers

1 How do I get my child to try new foods?

Start early! Research shows that introducing a child early to a wide range of foods means he or she is more likely to accept them. A child who is used to trying new things will continue to try new things, in most circumstances. Of course there will always be things that he or she doesn't like – but this is understandable and is the same with adults.

Delayed weaning, and delay in offering food with lumps and textures, can also be a cause of faddy eating and a limited range of foods in small children.

One UK study has found that the best way to offer small children a new food is in very small amounts, as part of a meal or varied snack. It is also wise to make sure that the child is hungry when trying new foods, so try to ensure they don't fill up in the hour or two before their meals with snacks or high-calorie drinks. They need to be hungry enough, but not *too* hungry, otherwise getting them to try new food will be difficult. Other research has found that you need to offer a new food up to ten times before the child may decide he or she likes it. Keep offering the rejected foods every couple of weeks or so. In time, your child may give them a go, so don't give up too soon!

Lastly, if children see you eating and enjoying a food they may be more inclined to give it a fair try. But being over stern with them or punishing them for refusal may compound the problem. Older children can be encouraged to try new foods by getting them to help you choose food in the shop and by helping you to prepare and cook it. They will also be helped by seeing other children enjoy those foods, so having kids round to tea who have an adventurous attitude to food will always be a help.

2 What makes a child suddenly turn fussy and refuse foods?

The Royal College of Psychiatrists says that food refusal or selective eating is 'a normal and common stage of development in pre-school children'. Up to a third of under-fives go through a stage of being fussy about food. This can take the form of refusing foods previously enjoyed, refusing all foods except a very few items, refusing any new foods, missing meals or taking a very long time to eat.

There may be several reasons for this behaviour. It could partly be the need of the child to exercise some influence over his or her life. Food is one of the few ways that a young child can express personality, and food refusal can be a good way to show emotions such as displeasure. Small children – usually around two or three years old – begin to realise that they can have an effect on their parents and begin to test how far they can go. Being fussy about food is also a good way to grab your attention.

Of course, all children have their favourite foods and foods that give them comfort and it is quite normal for them, at times, to want those foods and refuse others. They may be overtired, ill, teething, under stress – say, starting at nursery or picking up on a parental disagreement. For some children, once they have practised food refusal it can be hard for them to get out of the habit. If they are not underweight and seem healthy you should try not to worry too much. Becoming cross or visibly worried, or trying to force them to eat or punish them (perhaps by making them sit at the table until they have eaten) will probably make the situation worse. See the tips, below, on helping your children to enjoy their food.

However, the good news is that most children do outgrow being fussy. The best strategy, if you are worried about their health or nutrient intake, is to see your doctor; otherwise try to stay calm and relaxed and offer foods when the child seems most receptive and happy. Remember that all children will dislike certain foods, so try to build on the ones they do like. Food fads may be short-lived. It will also help if you make sure they are hungry at mealtimes – perhaps ensure they avoid items such as crisps, cakes or biscuits in between meals. And remember that many drinks are high in calories and will fill them up so that they aren't hungry enough to want to eat – milkshakes, fizzy drinks and even undiluted fruit juice can all dull appetite.

HELPING YOUR CHILD TO ENJOY HIS FOOD

- Don't make a fuss at mealtimes. Make sure meals are sociable occasions with no arguments.

- Be calm if your children refuse to eat something, and don't insist on a clean plate.

- Try to eat a few bites of the children's meal with them, or a little snack, even if you are planning a meal later. Children don't like to eat in isolation.

- Sometimes, children eat better when the portions are smaller. They can be put off when faced with a large plateful.

- Toddlers often eat better if they're allowed to feed themselves with their fingers, and not be spoon-fed.

- Children sometimes accept small tastes of alternatives from somebody else's plate even if they won't eat it on their own plate.

- Let the children get naturally hungry for their meal. It's best to avoid high-sugar, high-fat snacks in the hour or two before a meal.

- Too many high-calorie drinks in between meals can fill a child up.

- When introducing new foods, remember a 'taste' can be as small as half a teaspoon.

- Only offer one new food at a time and serve a new food with a familiar food.

- Children often enjoy brightly coloured foods with mild flavours and interesting textures, so go for these if your child is a fussy eater.

3 Can a child be healthy on a very limited diet of just a few items?

The answer to that question largely depends on what the items are. If a child were to eat, say, cheese and tomato sandwiches, milk and apples, he would get a much wider range of nutrients than a child eating just, say, crisps, chips, sandwiches and cola. In the short term all types of very selective eating may not be cause for great concern. There have been several documented cases of children on limited diets such as jam sandwiches and milk or bananas and orange juice who, when medically examined, proved to be in perfectly good health.

But if a child continues to eat only two or three foods for longer than a few weeks it is best to take him or her to the doctor for medical advice. In the long term a restricted diet can cause various symptoms, diseases and problems.

For instance, if a child gets no fruit or vegetables at all then he or she will lack vitamin C and could develop scurvy and immune system problems. Long term, a child without adequate calcium would suffer bone density or growth problems – and so on.

One thing we will say is that when parents write to Judith, our Diet Detective, with the complaint that their child will only eat a few things she finds, about 80% of the time, when she actually looks at the child's diet, that in fact he or she is getting a lot more variety than the parent realises.

When you have a child who seems to be existing on just a few foods, try all the advice given above for fussy eaters and food refusal.

4 How do I get my child to eat vegetables and other healthy foods?

Children are more likely to accept a range of vegetables if you begin offering them regularly after weaning. Many children have a few vegetables that they don't enjoy, often the very strong-tasting or bitter ones such as sprouts or chicory. But if you start early and make veggies part of most meals then there should be at least some that are eaten with relish, particularly the sweet ones such as carrots, squash, tomatoes and sweetcorn. If not, try the tips in the Box on the following page.

TIPS FOR GETTING MORE VEGETABLES IN YOUR CHILD'S DIET

- They are often enjoyed more if they're in a cheese sauce and/or with pasta and/or in an oven bake.

- Blended vegetable soups with bread and some grated cheese on top almost always go down well.

- Try a meat or chicken casserole or pie with added diced vegetables.

- Overcooked and soggy vegetables are a turn off for most children. Avoid boiling them – just lightly steam, bake, stir-fry or roast.

- Offer crudités. Surprisingly, children often enjoy crunching on crisp, fresh vegetables cut into strips to be eaten with the fingers, perhaps with a tasty dip.

- Try vegetable juices, such as carrot or tomato juice, as a change from fruit juices.

- Make a finely diced vegetable sauce to be served with pasta, rice or baked potatoes.

- Don't say 'no dessert until you've eaten up your vegetables'. This will not only make them think that veggies = punishment, but you are also giving them the idea that the pudding is more desirable than the vegetables.

5 Can I give my child supplements instead of fish?

It is almost always best if vitamins, minerals and other important nutrients can be provided naturally in the diet, but that isn't always possible. For example, if a child is vegan they will find it very hard to get enough vitamin B12 from their diet and supplements may be required. If your child refuses to eat fish, especially oily fish such as salmon, mackerel, fresh tuna, herrings or sardines, then he or she could be missing out on the vital omega-3 oils that they contain. Omega-3s have been strongly linked with various health and development benefits including brain-power and concentration. They can also help with eczema. They may also be important for heart health and many other conditions that can affect us as we get older. So it may well be worth giving your child a supplement if they don't regularly eat fish. You could give vegetarian children a spoonful of flaxseed oil or hemp oil every day – these also contain omega-3s. When giving fish oil supplements, try to buy brands low in toxin pollutants. Advice on this subject is available on the Netmums website.

6 What can I do about my child's poor appetite?

Several of the tips in the Box on page 14 may help to encourage a child to eat. Paradoxically, a child with a poor appetite, who needs to put on weight, is often best given very small platefuls – more regularly, if necessary. They often get very put off if asked to eat a large meal and may end up eating less than if they had been offered a very small portion. Also, the digestive system feels less bloated if large meals are avoided.

Little and often may be the key, and bright colours, fresh tastes and being able to pick at food – finger food – when they feel like it can also help. Plenty of exercise and fresh air may also help stimulate the appetite.

For older children, especially those who aren't underweight, you should also make sure that he or she isn't filling up between meals on snack items such as crisps, sweets and calorie-laden drinks. Even if you don't see them doing this, be aware that they may be spending their pocket money, or indulging at friends' houses. For thin children who need to put on weight but have a poor appetite, try between-meal snacks of fresh nuts (non-allergic children over five) and seeds, dried fruit and smoothies made with full-fat milk.

7 How do I stop my child putting on too much weight?

If a child is gaining too much weight you should first cut back on high-calorie between-meal drinks and snacks. Just by not providing him or her with crisps, biscuits, cakes, chocolate, sweets and fizzy drinks you may well find that your child slims down naturally and gradually over time, not least as he or she gets older and taller. If the child complains of hunger you should provide fresh fruit or a rice cake between meals.

If that isn't the problem you should offer smaller portions at each meal. If you reduce portion sizes by 25%, for example, then your child will be taking in 25% fewer calories and this should be enough to produce a slimmer figure over time.

Encourage your child to drink water rather than commercial drinks – and for children over five offer skimmed milk rather than full-fat or semi-skimmed. Just 500ml of skimmed milk a day will provide much of the calcium they need.

If a child is part of a whole family who tend to be overweight then you could cut back calories by reducing the fat content in family meals (see fat-cutting tips, page 30). Increase the proportion of vegetables/salad on the plate and decrease the amount of meat/carbohydrates a little. Avoid desserts except for those based on fresh fruit. Take more exercise as a family – weekend walks, cycle rides, that kind of thing.

8 How do I know what size portions to give my child?

If a child is average weight and eats up their meals then the portion sizes you are offering are probably just about right. If you offer meals and your average-weight child is always coming back for seconds then the portions may be a little small. If your child regularly leaves food on the plate then the portion sizes are probably too large for him or her. And if your child is overweight then you may be giving slightly large portion sizes, even though he or she eats up. See also question number seven, as other factors may be involved.

In general, children between seven and 10 may need as many, or nearly as many, calories per day as an adult female in order to maintain reasonable weight and grow, and certainly by 10 or 11 children should normally be eating adult-sized meals. So don't be surprised if your child of seven-plus can eat an adult-sized portion without putting on weight. But of course the child's height and activity levels need to be taken into account. A small, sedentary child won't need so many calories.

Portion sizes for fruit and vegetables for various ages appear in the Box below.

FRUIT AND VEGETABLE PORTION SIZES
For children aged 10-plus to adult

Fruit	A portion is:
Apple, medium banana, pear, orange	1
Plums, fresh apricots and similar medium fruits	2
Grapefruit, avocado, mango	1/2
Melon	1 average slice
Pineapple	2 rings
Fruit salad or tinned fruit in juice	3 tbsp
Stewed, fresh or dried fruit	3 tbsp
Grapes, cherries, berries	80g
Dried fruits	1 heaped tbsp
Fruit juice or fruit smoothie	150ml
Vegetables	
Small/chunks cooked veg	3 tbsp
Green leafy veg	4 tbsp
Salad	1 large breakfast/dessert bowl
Pulses, cooked	3 tbsp

For children aged one to three

A quarter to a third of these quantities is approximately a portion.

For children aged three to six

Half these quantities is approximately a portion.

For children aged six to 10

Increase the portion sizes gradually so that by 10 years old they are eating full-sized portions.

GETTING FIVE A DAY

- Adults and children should eat at least five portions of fruit and vegetables a day.

- Fruits in between the size of a plum and an apple, e.g. a satsuma or kiwi, can be considered as a full portion for most children.

- Only one glass of fruit juice a day can count towards the five-a-day, no matter how much is consumed.

- To count towards the five-a-day the portions should be of the size stated above.

- Children should vary the types of fruit and veg they eat for maximum benefit and should aim for at least two to three portions of veg a day, rather than taking their five-a-day all as fruit.

9 Is it OK to give a child between-meal snacks?

Yes, when children are active or working hard at school they usually need a couple of between-meal snacks to keep them going – say, mid-morning and when they get home from school.

The crux is what type of snack you give them. It is best to avoid offering high-saturated or trans fat, high-salt, high-sugar commercial items on a regular basis as these types of snack tend to be low on nutrients. Good snacks will provide lasting energy and some useful nutrients. Some good 'swaps' appear in the Box on the following page.

Also, if you are providing a healthy breakfast that contains some complex carbohydrates, some fat and some protein, children will be able to keep going until lunchtime without feeling the need for a quick sugar fix. And, similarly, if they have a healthy lunch they will be less inclined to grab the doughnuts when they get home from school. Of course, if you haven't bought the doughnuts in the first place, this will help them to make the right choices.

So, think of between-meal snacks as a chance to offer children small amounts of good quality 're-fuelling' material, packed full of the nutrients that they need.

SWAPS	
Bag of crisps	Small handful of fresh nuts (for children over five, e.g. almonds, Brazils, cashews)
Tube or box of sweets or a chocolate bar	Small bag you have made up yourself, including a few chocolate chips, a few pieces of dried fruit and a few nuts
Slice of white bread and jam	Rice cake topped with a little peanut butter (also see Allergies pages 36–7)
Slice of jam and cream sponge cake	Slice of fruit loaf (see page 208)

10 What is the best drink for my child?

From weaning (six months) to 12 months the best drink for children is breast or formula milk – 600ml a day. Cooled boiled water can also be offered.

From one to two years old whole milk and water are the only drinks a child needs. From three to five you can offer semi-skimmed milk and water and over five, skimmed milk can be given.

Fruit juices are best offered diluted, as the acids they contain may damage tooth enamel and the sugars they contain may contribute to tooth decay and gum disease. They are also high in calories and should be limited for children prone to weight problems. It is best to offer whole fruit and water to children rather than fruit juice.

Fruit smoothies made with the whole fruit, yoghurt or milk are ideal drinks for occasional use as they contain a range of nutrients including calcium, fibre and vitamin C. But they can be high in calories.

Commercial drinks containing sugar, flavourings, colourings and acids are best avoided or given only occasionally. Fizzy drinks and squashes are linked with obesity, possible behaviour problems and tooth and gum disease. Drinks containing artificial sweeteners may be lower in calories but do nothing to discourage a sweet tooth and high intake of some of these sweeteners by children is not advised.

The basics of healthy eating for kids

The recipes in this book will help you to serve nutritious, tasty and interesting main meals, light meals and quick food ideas for your children at any time of year. It is important for kids to have a healthy diet. Food provides the calories for growth and energy but also provides amino acids for muscle development, essential fats for proper functioning and development, and a range of vitamins, minerals and chemicals for disease protection and long-term health.

Nutrition: A Crash Course

We now know that a good, balanced diet can help protect children from obesity, diabetes, heart disease, cancers and other major ills, and can help brain development, protect bones, boost the immune system, avoid obesity, and even affect behaviour and mood. And most of us know at least something about healthy eating, but there is a lot of conflicting advice in the press every day about what they should and shouldn't be getting. So here are some notes to help you provide your children with a balanced diet.

You'll find a clear description of the various nutrients that all children need, then a rundown of the items you should go easy on, such as salt and sugar. Lastly there are plenty of tips for providing healthy food quickly, and at low cost.

Although the optimum diet varies slightly according to the age of your child, the basic nutrients children need are summed up below.

Calories

Calories, or kilocalories as they are correctly known, are the units that measure the amount of energy in the food we eat. All food – carbohydrate, fat, protein – that kids eat and drink contains calories. Only water is calorie-free. And while we do need to keep a watch on total calorie consumption, most children do need a lot of calories to provide them with energy to grow, exercise, play, work and repair themselves. An average seven- to 10-year-old child needs as many calories as an average adult woman.

Carbohydrates

Carbohydrate-rich foods provide the most easily absorbed form of energy for children and are ideal for instant, short-term and medium-term energy. Carbohydrates divide into two main groups: starches, e.g. wheat, oats and other grains, root vegetables such as potatoes, and pulses like lentils; and sugars, e.g. fruits, some vegetables, honey, sugar and, in manufactured produce, extracted forms of sugar.

Children should eat most of their carbohydrates in the form of starches, as well as some sugars via fruit and vegetables. As children get older they should get more and more of their starches in the form of 'whole' foods, i.e. whole grains (brown rice, wholegrain bread, wholewheat pasta, etc.). The highly refined carbs of processed foods are generally less satisfying and less good for the digestive system than whole carbs. Ideally, only a small part of their carbohydrate intake should come from sugar and processed sugary foods and drinks.

Protein

Your child's muscle and organs such as the heart are built using protein. Protein also provides the tools for body maintenance and repair.

The main sources of protein in our children's diet are meat, dairy produce, eggs, poultry, fish, pulses, nuts and seeds. Many carbohydrate foods, such as potatoes and whole grains, also contain protein. Average daily requirements for protein are:

Age one to three: **14.5g**
Age four to six: **20g**
Age seven to 10: **28g**
Age 11: **42g**

These amounts are usually easily met in the average western diet: e.g. 300ml (10fl oz) semi-skimmed milk contains around 10g protein; one small portion of chicken breast contains around 22g protein; and one egg about 7g.

Fat

Fat is a great source of medium- and long-term energy for children. Fat, gram for gram, contains twice the calories of carbohydrate or protein. It takes longer to be absorbed into the bloodstream than carbs and so is ideal to keep children's energy up over a long day or for a long sports session. Fat also provides the fat-soluble vitamins A, D, E and K. But not all fat is equal!

Children should get most of their fat in the form of *mono-unsaturated* and *polyunsaturated* fats, with only small amounts of fat in the form of *saturated* fat and preferably no *trans* fats. See the box below for an explanation of these different fats and where to find them. An ideal total daily fat intake for children under five is around 40% of their total calorie intake. Over five it is around 30–35%.

FAT TYPES

Mono-unsaturated fats

Healthy fats found in the highest quantities in olive, rapeseed and groundnut oils, avocados and nuts.

Health notes: Can help to maintain a healthy heart and arteries.

Polyunsaturated fats

This group contains the essential fats, linoleic acid (an omega-6 fat) and alpha-linolenic acid (an omega-3 fat). Good sources of linoleic acid are most nut and seed oils, nuts and seeds. Good sources of alpha-linolenic acid are flaxseed oil, walnut oil, groundnut oil and hempseed oil. The group also contains the long-chain omega-3 fats DHA and EPA found mainly in oily fish.

Health notes: Polyunsaturated fats are, on the whole, good for heart health. The health benefits are more dubious, though, for certain types of polyunsaturates such as corn oil and sunflower oil. These change when exposed to high temperatures and once heated they act more like saturated fats in the body. Essential fats are ideally consumed cold.

Saturated fats

Found mainly in fatty animal produce, e.g. fatty cuts of meat, high-fat dairy produce, butter, pastry and commercial bakes.

Health notes: High intake is a risk factor for heart disease, and more and more children are showing signs of blocked arteries.

Trans fats

Found in commercial products such as bakes, biscuits, cakes, desserts, which contain polyunsaturated fats that have been hydrogenated (chemically altered).

Health notes: Trans fats are probably the worst types of fats to consume and are best avoided. They are linked with arterial damage and weight gain.

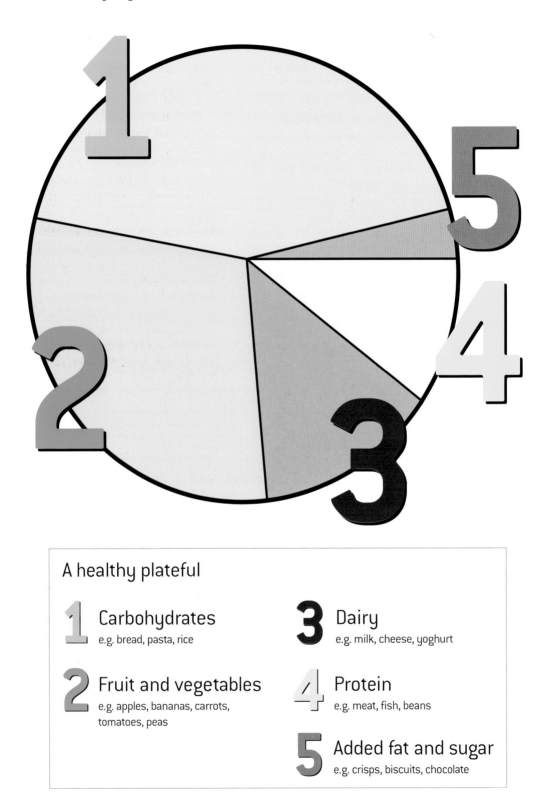

A healthy plateful

1 Carbohydrates
e.g. bread, pasta, rice

3 Dairy
e.g. milk, cheese, yoghurt

2 Fruit and vegetables
e.g. apples, bananas, carrots, tomatoes, peas

4 Protein
e.g. meat, fish, beans

5 Added fat and sugar
e.g. crisps, biscuits, chocolate

Vitamins and minerals

Vitamins are essential organic compounds, which humans need in very small quantities to maintain health. Minerals are inorganic elements also vital for human functioning. To ensure that children get a complete range of these and don't fall short, the best advice is to offer a varied balanced diet containing plenty of natural foods. Vitamin C and the B group vitamins need to be eaten regularly as the body can't store them.

Phytochemicals

Natural foods, such as vegetables, fruits, nuts and seeds, contain thousands of plant chemicals that appear to be as important for health, disease protection and growth as the well-known vitamins and minerals. They include groups called flavonoids, polyphenols, carotenoids, catechins, glucosinolates, and many more. The best insurance against children missing out on any of these vital compounds is to ensure they eat up their fruit and vegetables and get a wide variety.

A balanced diet

The plate pictured opposite represents a good daily balance of foods for your child aged over two.

To ensure health, the UK Food Standards Agency says we should *all* (over age two) be eating:

- more fruit and veg.
- more starchy foods such as rice, bread, pasta (try to choose wholegrain varieties when you can) and potatoes.
- less fat, salt and sugar.
- some protein-rich foods such as meat, fish, eggs and pulses.
- a variety of foods to ensure the full range of nutrients.

We should also be drinking around 1.2 litres (2 pints) fluid a day plus fluid in food.

Cutting Down On...

Good nutrition isn't just about what our children *do* eat – it's also about cutting down on the unhealthy foods. Most of our children tend to eat too much salt, sugar, certain types of fats, and artificial additives.

Salt

Babies only need a very small amount of salt – a one-year-old baby for example should not eat more than 1g of salt a day. Remember not to add salt to food you give to your baby because their kidneys can't cope with any extra salt. And be careful not to give your baby processed foods that aren't made specifically for babies, such as breakfast cereals and pasta sauces, because these can be high in salt.

There is also no need to add salt to your child's food. If you're buying processed foods, even those aimed at children, remember to check the information given on the labels so that you can choose those with less salt.

• When reading labels remember that sodium is not the same as salt. Salt is sodium chloride containing 40% sodium and 60% chloride. Therefore to find the salt when only sodium is given you need to multiply it by 2.5. For example, a product contains 400mg of sodium per portion: it therefore contains 1000mg salt (1g).

• These are the maximum amounts of salt children should have in a day – research indicates that many children exceed these amounts:

seven to 12 months:
less than 1g a day salt (0.4g sodium)

one to three years:
2g a day (0.8g sodium)

four to six years:
3g salt a day (1.2g sodium)

seven to 10 years:
5g a day (2g sodium)

11 and over:
6g a day (2.5g sodium)

Here are a few practical tips to help you cut down your salt intake:

• Check the labels on processed foods such as soups and ready meals. Choose those with less added salt or sodium.

• Add less salt to your cooking.

• Get out of the habit of adding salt to your food. Try to remember to taste it first.

• Cut down on salty snacks such as crisps and nuts, and heavily salted foods such as bacon, cheese, pickles and smoked fish.

• Choose canned vegetables, pulses and fish that say 'no added salt'.

• Choose lower-salt stock cubes, make your own stock, or add herbs and spices for flavour instead.

• Cut down on sauces, such as cooking sauces, soy sauce, Worcestershire sauce, brown sauce and ketchup, because these are usually very high in salt.

Sugar

The recommended maximum amount of sugar a child should eat a day is:

one to three years:
31g (boys), 29g (girls)

four to six years:
43g (boys), 39g (girls)

seven to 10 years:
49g (boys), 43g (girls)

High-sugar items

50g bar chocolate (around 29g sugar)
50g sweets (around 47g sugar)
500ml bottle cola (around 55g sugar)
200ml fruit juice drink (around 20g sugar)
50g slice chocolate fudge cake (around 23g sugar)
50g cluster-type breakfast cereal (around 18g sugar)

Use these tips to help your children eat less sugar:

• Give them fewer sugary drinks and snacks.

• Instead of fizzy drinks and juice drinks, go for water or diluted unsweetened fruit juice. If it is hard to wean them from fizzy drinks then try diluting fruit juice with sparkling water.

• Instead of cakes or biscuits, try giving them a currant bun, a crumpet, a slice of melon or some malt loaf with low-fat spread, or try the snack recipes in this book. Buns, crumpets and malt loaf are sold with the breads in supermarkets as they contain much less sugar and fat than most cakes and are a little more filling for a snack than a piece of fruit if a child has, say, come home from football and is ravenous.

• If your children take sugar in hot drinks, or add sugar to breakfast cereal, gradually reduce the amount until they can cut it out altogether.

• Rather than spreading high sugar jam, marmalade, syrup, treacle or honey on toast, try a low-fat spread (for children over five), sliced banana, or low-fat cream cheese instead.

• Check food labels to help you pick the foods with less added sugar, or go for the low-sugar version.

• Try halving the sugar you use in your recipes. It works for most things except jam, meringues and ice-cream.

• Choose cans of fruit in juice rather than syrup.

• Choose wholegrain breakfast cereals rather than those coated with sugar or honey.

• Sugar can be hard to spot in children's food, as it's called many different things. All the following are forms of sugar: sucrose, glucose, fructose, maltose, dextrose, fruit syrup, molasses.

Fat

Use these tips to help control the fat intake for children over five, particularly their intake of saturated and trans fats.

• Choose lean cuts of meat and trim off any visible fat.

• Grill, bake, poach or steam sometimes rather than fry and roast, so you don't need to add any extra fat.

• If you do choose something high in fat for them to eat, such as a meat pie, pick something low in fat to go with it to make the meal lower in fat overall. For example, give them a baked potato instead of chips.

• When you're choosing a ready meal or snack, compare the labels so you can pick those with less saturated fat and total fat.

• Put some extra vegetables, beans or lentils in your casseroles and stews and a bit less meat.

• Measure oil for cooking with tablespoons or teaspoons rather than pouring it straight from a container.

• Have pies with only one crust rather than two – either a lid or a base, not both – because pastry is very high in fat.

• When you make sandwiches using butter, make sure it is at room temperature so that you can spread it more thinly.

• Choose lower-fat versions of dairy foods whenever you can. This means semi-skimmed or skimmed milk, reduced-fat yoghurt, lower-fat cheeses or very strong tasting cheese, so you don't need to use as much.

• Instead of cream or soured cream, try using yoghurt or fromage frais, e.g. with fruits salads or fruit pies.

• Try to cut down on the amount of snack foods and commercial baked goods that you buy. These are often the items high in saturates or trans fats.

Healthy Food, Fast Food

We are often asked how it's possible to produce healthy food without spending too much time in the kitchen and without buying ready and convenience meals. Here are some tips:

• Base meals around pasta – semi-wholewheat is healthy and takes no longer to cook than the white variety. Some ready-made sauces are very good quality; check out the chilled counter as, generally, chilled-counter items will contain less salt and have a better nutrient profile than similar items found in jars and cans and dried packs because they are fresher.

• Bulgar wheat and couscous are two very fast alternative starches to pasta.

• Cook brown rice and freeze it in batches. It will defrost in a few minutes.

• Never make your own sauce for pasta, meat, fish, etc. without doubling or quadrupling quantities – freeze the extra in batches.

• Most egg-based meals are quick and easy. Think of omelette, scrambled eggs, tortilla.

• Make the most of ready-prepared salads. Although they contain fewer vitamins and plant chemicals than fresh whole salad stuff, they still contain good amounts.

• Grill meat, chicken and fish in small pieces to save time. A quick marinade, e.g. lemon juice and crushed garlic or light soy sauce and olive oil, will tenderise them.

• From April to October don't worry if you serve up cold dinners – salads are nutritious and filling.

• Stir-fries are a great standby and very healthy, but go easy on packet sauces with a high salt content (see page 58). See also note on salt on page 28.

• Get the family to help you. Children enjoy helping.

Healthy Low-Cost Food

It's generally thought that healthy food costs a lot more than junk food but this really doesn't have to be the case. Here is a list of some of our favourite low-cost healthy foods with tips on how to save costs even more:

• Fresh fruit and vegetables in season. Shop at local markets. You can buy in bulk and share produce with neighbours or freeze extra.

• Brown rice, pasta, baking potatoes and bread are some of the lowest cost and healthiest foods you can find.

• Pulses – such as green and brown lentils, chickpeas, red kidney beans and cannellini beans – are a great source of protein, carbohydrate, fibre, vitamins and minerals and are very low cost indeed. Canned or dried, they are great value.

• Eggs are full of nutrients and organic eggs tend to have a higher concentration of omega-3 fats than battery eggs and don't cost a lot more.

• Canned fish such as mackerel, sardines and tuna are all quite inexpensive. Buy the types canned in good-quality oil or spring water or tomato sauce. Avoid those canned in brine, because of the high salt content.

• Canned tomatoes and tomato products such as passata, tomato purée and sauces are all rich in lycopene – a form of carotene, a plant chemical which helps protect health – and low in fat.

Food Labelling

Do you know what is in the food you eat? If you think that your bread is simply made of flour and yeast, take a look at the label and see how many unpronounceable, chemical-sounding names have been included.

When faced with the massive choice of yoghurts in the supermarkets, do you tend to opt for the ones with the cartoon characters assuming that they must be healthy if they are aimed at children?

It may take a bit of time and practice at first, but learning to read food labels can be a massive step towards getting your family eating healthily.

The Traffic Light System is a way of food labelling that helps to show customers whether the items they have to choose from are low, medium or high in fat, saturates, sugars and salt. Some supermarkets have adopted or are adopting this system. The following table shows what the guidelines mean:

	Green less than	Amber	Red more than
Fat	3g/100g	more than 3 and less than 20g/100g	20g/100g
Saturates	1.5g/100g	more than 0.5 and less than 5g/100g	5g/100g
Total Sugars	5g/100g	more than 5 and less than 15g/100g	15g/100g
Salt	0.3g/100g	more than 0.3 and less than 1.5g/100g	1.5g/100g

We have adapted this Traffic Light System to give an idea of the levels of fats, saturates, sugars and salt in the recipes in this book.

Other labels carry different types of nutritional information but, at the moment, labelling is still largely voluntary unless specific health claims are made for the food. For example, if it is claimed on the front of the pack that the food is 'low in fat' then the amount of fat in the food must be clearly stated.

While some countries are obliged to show trans fat content, in the UK there is currently no requirement to do so, which makes avoiding trans fats quite difficult. In this case you should check the ingredients label for 'hydrogenated fat' or 'trans fats' or 'partially hydrogenated fat'.

Ingredients on food labels

The listing of ingredients on food labels is compiled by law in order of amount, with the highest first down to the lowest. For instance, if the first ingredient is sugar, then the product has more sugar than any other ingredient. So you can get a good idea of what your food contains by looking at this list.

Additives

Many parents try to avoid buying products with artificial colorants, flavourings, preservatives, etc. These are usually listed as E numbers. There is research that shows that certain additives have adverse effects on children, e.g. hyperactivity, lowered concentration and allergies. It has been shown that the foods that contain the highest levels of these additives are also those likely to be highest in fat, sugar and salt.

The good news is that due to these consumer concerns, the supermarkets seem to be leaning on manufacturers to reduce the number and extent of additives used in their products. So, if you are worried, vote with your purse. It really does work – you *can* make a difference. Here are some of the additives it may be wise to avoid because they have caused most reported problems in children:

Colours
Tartrazine (E102)
Sunset Yellow (E110)
Carmoisine (E122)
Ponceau 4R (E124)

Preservatives
Sodium Benzoate (E211)
Other benzoates (E210–219)

Sulphides (E220–228)
Nitrates and nitrites (E249–E252)

Flavour enhancers
Monosodium glutamate and other
glutamates (E621–E623)

Antioxidants
E310–E312, E320, E321

ADDITIVES IN FOODS			
Additive category	Reason for use	Their E numbers	Used in
Colours	Make the product look more attractive or more like the natural counterpart; restore colour lost in processing	E100–E180	Soft drinks, desserts, cakes, sweets, snacks, crisps, very many products
Flavourings	Add flavour to a bland product, add aroma	E100–E180	See above. As colours – used very widely in processed foods and drinks
Flavour enhancers [e.g. monosodium glutamate]	Improve flavour in processed foods	E620–640	See flavourings. [e.g. monosodium glutamate], also takeaway foods
Preservatives	Prolong product life; prevent bacteria that may cause food poisoning	E200–285, E1105	Processed meats, ambient products [those stored at room temperature], dried fruits, many products
Sweeteners [intense artificial sweeteners and bulking agents]	Add sweetness, make more palatable , add bulk, reduce energy content	E420, E421, E953–959	Drinks, desserts, yoghurts, and many products
Emulsifiers, stabilisers, thickeners	Prevent separation, enhance texture	E322–E495	Desserts, soups, sauces, shakes, and more
Antioxidants	Prevent fatty food going rancid	E300–321	Fats, fat-containing foods
Others	Flour improvers, bleaches, processing aids, glazes and others	E500–578, E901–914, E920–926, E999–1518	Wide range of processed foods

Allergies

If statistics are to be believed, food allergy is rising fast and about 5% of children under the age of four have a food allergy, whilst the figure is less than half that in adults. Most childhood food allergies are outgrown by school age. Food intolerance is perhaps less serious but also less easy to diagnose. It can have more unpredictable outcomes than a food allergy and the symptoms may be milder. Here are some facts and tips to help you cope with the problem.

• Nut allergy or peanut (groundnut) allergy is one of the most common and is very rarely outgrown, so, once diagnosed, nuts should be avoided throughout life. Some children are allergic to peanuts but not other nuts.

• Coeliac disease is an allergy to gluten in grains, is lifelong and needs specialist help.

• Lactose intolerance is intolerance to the sugars in milk and may become less severe with age and treatment.

• The top foods (allergens) most likely to cause allergic reactions in children are: cow's milk, peanuts, other nuts, eggs, soya milk, soya products, wheat, sesame seeds, fish and shellfish.

• Strawberries and citrus fruits may produce heat rashes and other reactions in susceptible children.

• Children with one or more parents who have a food allergy, asthma or eczema are be more likely to contract an allergy.

• Breastfeeding may offer protection but mothers who already have an allergy, asthma or eczema, should avoid eating the foods most likely to cause problems during pregnancy and breastfeeding.

• Babies and small children at risk should not be given known allergenic foods.

• For susceptible infants, weaning should not start until six months.

• Anaphylactic shock is a severe and immediate reaction. It is rare but can be life-threatening and peanuts are the leading cause. In any case, peanuts should not be fed to children under one year.

• For high-risk children, wait until they are at least three before trying them with nut butters.

• If you suspect your child has a food allergy you should see your doctor for further advice.

• You should find comprehensive allergy information on product labels, which will help you avoid buying foods which contain, or are likely to contain, any known allergens. And you should be able to obtain details of own-brand foods that are free from allergens from all major supermarkets.

ORGANIC OR NOT?

While the label 'organic' does not necessarily mean that the product you buy will taste nicer, has been cooked to a better recipe, or will be better for your health or your children's health than a non-organic equivalent, sometimes it may.

There has been some research in recent years to show that organic fruit and vegetables do often contain higher levels of various vitamins, minerals and plant chemicals than intensively produced equivalents. And organic fruit and veg do often contain more flavour, a subjective but very common view.

If you buy UK organic produce with the Soil Association label, then you are almost certainly getting a product that has been produced from conception to the shop floor with care. It won't contain additives, preservatives, antibiotic and hormone residues that can be found in non-organic versions.

In the UK we can't produce enough organic food to satisfy demand, so the majority of organics come from abroad where controls may be less rigorous.

Perhaps rather than choosing sometimes dubious organic imports, try to buy 'traceable' food grown or farmed in your own area. Visit local farm shops, local small town traders, farmers' markets and WI markets. Buy food in season and even try growing your own instead of flowers. Children love to see food grow. Even a few pots on a windowsill or patio would be a step in the right direction.

Meal planning

Planning what your family are going to eat for the few days ahead can make the difference between serenely sailing through your week and jumping from one day to the next, panicking about what to put on the table that night. The latter often involves diving into the supermarket for some frozen pizzas or, worse, hitting the takeaway because you've run out of steam.

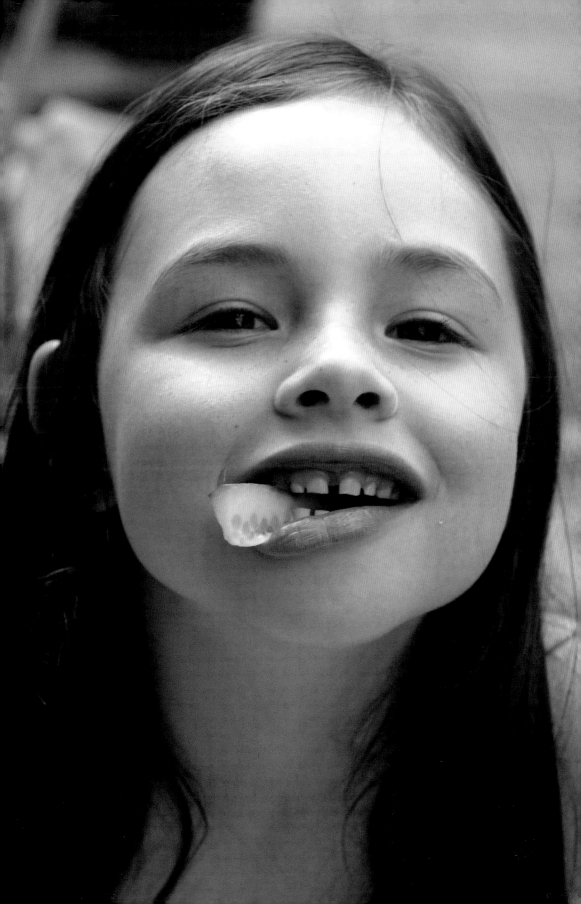

Incorporate your children's favourites into this simple planner, below, and perhaps aim to include a couple of new dishes each week. When planning evening meals bear in mind what your children have had during the rest of the day. If possible, find out what they ate for school lunch. If they had, say, a beefburger for lunch then don't give them beef (in any form) in the evening. If they had egg sandwiches for lunch, don't give them omelette in the evening.

Consider using a supermarket delivery service or local veg scheme; once you've planned your meals: it's quick and easy to place your order, and you are far less likely to get tempted by anything unhealthy. Using a meal planner chart like the one shown here can save your sanity. It really does make a difference. You can download a printable version from the Netmums website.

	MONDAY	TUESDAY	WEDNESDAY	THURSDAY	FRIDAY
WEEK 1					
WEEK 2					
WEEK 3					
WEEK 4					

Breakfast

Every child should start the day with a good breakfast. It doesn't have to be large; it doesn't have to be cooked; it doesn't have to take more than a minute or two to prepare. All research shows that breakfast is a very important meal for children and helps them to work better at school. A good breakfast will also help stop the urge to nibble and snack on less healthy items during the morning. A good breakfast should contain:

• Some protein, e.g. milk, yoghurt, egg, nuts, ham.

• Some good-quality unsweetened carbohydrate, e.g. wholegrain cereal, bread.

• A little fat, e.g. in whole milk, whole yoghurt, nuts, seeds, butter, eggs.

• Some vitamin C, preferably in fresh fruit.

Here are some examples of good breakfasts:

• Weetabix topped with milk and sliced fresh fruit; slice of bread with butter and honey.

• Boiled egg, slice of wholemeal bread, satsuma.

• Yoghurt and fruit smoothie (see pages 200–3).

• Muesli (for children over five without nut allergy), fresh fruit, milk.

• Yoghurt topped with fresh and dried fruit and a little oats or muesli.

• Porridge with a little sugar and milk, fresh fruit.

Lunch

If you send your child to school with a packed lunch you will find plenty of good ideas in Chapter 7. An ideal packed lunch will contain a similar balance of nutrients to breakfast, i.e. some protein, carbohydrate, a little fat and some vitamin C. The ideal drink is water or milk or diluted fruit juice.

A Week of Lunchbox Ideas

MONDAY	TUESDAY	WEDNESDAY	THURSDAY	FRIDAY
• Sandwich of soft brown bread filled with *almost instant tuna spread* (page 160), tomato slices and cress • Small bag of mixed dried fruit • 1 fruit yoghurt or plain yoghurt with honey • *1 easy oaty biscuit* (page 218) • Orange juice diluted half and half with water	• 1 white pitta bread filled with *hummus* (page 156) and mixed chopped salad items of choice • 1 slice *fruit cake* (page 207) • 1 small apple • 1 fruit smoothie (page 200)	• *Pasta salad* (chicken included) (page 176) • Satsuma • *Fruit and nut cookie* (page 219) • Fruit fromage frais • Water	• *Cheesey beany wrap* (page 162) • *Carrot cake muffin* (page 214) • Fruit salad (ready-made or pack your own mix in a lidded waterproof container) • *Vegetable crisps* (page 174) • Milk (semi-skimmed or whole)	• Soft white bap filled with sliced hard-boiled egg, lettuce, cress and low-fat mayonnaise • Kiwi fruit or plum • 1 slice *five-cup fruit loaf* (page 208) • 1 individual tub low-fat rice pudding • Water

If your child has school lunches it is wise to try to get a rapport going with your child so that you know exactly what he or she has eaten at lunchtime. It is a good idea to visit the school and find out what they normally have on the menu – some schools are better than others at providing healthy foods. Some schools will even provide the day's menu on their website. It is never easy to make sure that your child chooses an ideal lunch and then actually eats it, so if your child has to rely on school lunches it is important to make sure that their evening meal is nutritious.

For lunches at home you can use some of the ideas from Chapter 7, or consider one of the lunches below.

• Poached or scrambled egg on white or wholemeal toast followed by fresh fruit.

• Low-salt baked beans or cheese on toast with fresh fruit.

• Baked potato with any of the toast toppings (see pages 82–3).

• Open sandwich of tasty bread topped with lean meat, poultry or canned fish and plenty of chopped salad.

• Cold pasta or couscous mixed with chopped salad vegetables and tuna or mozzarella.

Main meal/Tea

For many children teatime (or supper) is usually the main meal of the day, and as such it needs to be a good, satisfying, nutritious meal to last them through the rest of the evening and overnight. Here are some tips.

• Each main meal should contain some protein, e.g. meat, fish, eggs, cheese, pulses; some carbohydrate, e.g. potato, rice, pasta; and plenty of vegetables or salad.

• Try to balance any dessert with what has gone before. With a heavier main course, such as a pie or baked pasta dish, then serve a light dessert such as fruit.

• When planning your own meals for the week try to vary the elements of your main meals from day to day. A good plan would be:

    chicken or turkey once a week

    red meat once a week

    an egg or vegetarian dish once a week

    white fish once a week

    oily fish once a week

• Pasta and rice dishes can be part of any of the above e.g. pasta with meat sauce, rice with a chicken curry.

A Month of Meals

Here is a sample month of main meals using both the recipes in this book and simple no-recipe meals. Weekends are not included, as you may want to eat out, eat with friends or get your partner to cook a surprise!

	Monday	Tuesday
Week 1	Simple home-made burgers and chips (pages 86–7) Peas or sweetcorn Bananas and custard	Easy carbonara (page 71) Side salad of mixed leaves and cucumber Fruit salad
Week 2	Basic cheese and tomato pizza (pages 75–6) Side salad Apple slices and raisins	Spaghetti bolognese (page 70) Rhubarb fool (page 180)
Week 3	Kedgeree (page 65) Ice-cream and fresh fruit	Baked potato with low-salt baked beans and grated cheese Kiwi fruit
Week 4	Grilled pork sausages Mashed potato and low-salt baked beans Fruit salad and low-fat crème fraîche	Shepherd's pie (pages 135–6) Broccoli Pear

Wednesday	Thursday	Friday
Mild chicken curry (page 151) Basmati rice, with mango chutney Sliced bananas	Fishcakes (pages 52–4) Green beans and tomatoes Fruit yoghurt	Classic Spanish omelette (page 79) Potato wedges (page 104) and peas Quick cheesecake (page 182)
Fish fingers (Variations, page 48) Oven chips and low-salt baked beans Satsuma	Roast chicken Carrots, green beans and roast potatoes Basic apple crumble (page 194) with low-fat crème fraîche	Yummy vegetable lasagne (page 128) Side salad Fruit yoghurt
Tuna pasta bake (page 126) Side salad Grapes	Chilli con carne (page 152) Basmati rice and lettuce Fruit yoghurt	Simple chicken and vegetable stir-fry (page 62) Noodles Apple, oat and sultana muffins (page 215)
Macaroni cheese (page 73) Side salad Baked apples (page 191)	Chicken nuggets (pages 48–9) Corned beef hash browns (pages 56–7) and grilled tomatoes Smoothies (pages 200–3)	Grilled salmon steak New potatoes and peas Sweet pancakes (page 192) with fresh fruit

Easy teas and simple suppers

Teatime or suppertime is important for so many reasons. This is often our children's main meal of the day and the only main meal during school days when we have control over what goes on the plate and in their mouths. After a busy day most children are at their hungriest around 5–6pm and at their most receptive to whatever you have to offer.

Apart from a bedtime snack or milk drink, it's also the meal that is going to see them through the night, so it needs to be nutritious and the kind of meal that won't have them feeling hungry again in an hour or two.

But unfortunately for many of us parents, especially working mums or mums with children of a wide age-range, this can be our busiest and most stressful time of day – dealing with tired toddlers, meeting older children from various schools, taking them to friends' houses, collecting them from after-school clubs or all arriving home from swimming tired and hungry.

This chapter offers recipes for simple yet nutritious meals that don't take huge amounts of time, effort, money or skill to prepare. Many can be served from scratch in 20 minutes or less. We've avoided meals you need to prepare earlier and then cook, as we're assuming often tea is a last-minute thing, and we've avoided things that you can prepare quickly but then need a long cooking time – again, assuming you need the tea done *now*!

Have a look through the recipes, and get the kids to have a look too. If they pick something they like the sound of, you might just get some help with the preparation and get that tea on the table even more quickly.

Perennial favourites

There are some meals that get asked for time and time again by all kids. In this section we've bought together these perennial favourites, all of which are so easy to prepare and yet bring comfort and sustenance at any time of year.

Chicken nuggets

'Every day I get the question, "What are we having for tea, Mum?" and I still get the best reaction when I say, "Chicken nuggets and chips"! When you make them yourself there is no guilt involved. They have a lovely fun tea they can eat with their fingers and I know they've had a good home-cooked meal. Everybody's happy, and that doesn't happen too often!

'When I make home-made fish fingers and chips I serve them in little cones made of rolled up newspaper with kitchen roll inside. Just add the sound of the sea for a traditional seaside supper!' Christine, mum to Lauren and Callum

This recipe can also very easily be adapted for fish fingers by swapping the chicken breast for equivalent white fish fillet (e.g. cod), cut into finger-sized pieces. Fish can be fresh or frozen and thawed, approx. 450g.

Serves 2–4 children

Suitable for ages 1 year +

❄ **You can freeze after step 4, so long as the chicken hasn't been previously frozen**

Nutrition ⬤ Fat ⬤ Saturates ⬤ Sugar ⬤ Salt

2 large chicken breast fillets, skin removed

2–3 slices stale white or brown bread

2–3 tbsp plain flour

1 medium egg, beaten and thinned with a little milk

a little light olive oil

1 Preheat the grill or the oven to 180°C/350°F/Gas 4.

2 Cut the chicken into bite-sized chunks or into strips for chicken fingers. Remove the crusts and whiz the bread in a blender to make crumbs (or crumb, using your fingertips), then tip them into a shallow bowl.

NUTRITION NOTE

Chicken breast is an ideal low-saturated fat protein for children. It is easily digested and is rich in most of the B vitamin group. It's also a great source of selenium, a mineral lacking in many kids' diets. If the nuggets are grilled or baked they stay low in fat. If you shallow-fry, use light olive oil or safflower oil, not blended vegetable oil.

SERVING SUGGESTION

Serve with vegetable hash browns or potato wedges (see pages 57 and 104), or just plain mash with mixed peas and carrots.

3 Put the flour and chicken in a large strong plastic bag and shake to coat the chicken. Now dip the nuggets into the egg mixture to coat, and finally into the breadcrumbs.

4 Gently brush with a little oil and cook under the medium hot grill for 10–12 minutes, turning once. Or bake in the preheated oven for 15–20 minutes, turning once. Or, don't brush with oil, but shallow-fry for a similar time then drain on kitchen paper.

Variations

Substitute the chicken with cod, haddock or salmon slices and make fish fingers with the same crumb mixture. The fish versions may take a little less cooking time. You could also use chunks of turkey breast.

Netmums member Ffion from Cardiff, who sent in the recipe, says: 'Make this dish *even healthier* by adding *flaxseeds* or *chopped sunflower seeds* or *pine kernels* to the breadcrumb mixture for children over five (see Allergies, page 36). This gives it a *nice nutty flavour* and a bit of *crunchiness* – but don't overcook the bread coating as this will destroy the good omega oils in the seeds and may make them bitter. It's a *hit every time with my kids*, who can't stand the ready-made ones now!'

'You can *freeze home-made breadcrumbs* in plastic bags and they take *only minutes* to defrost.' Jenni, Colchester

'These are *very easy* to do in big batches so you can freeze what you don't need on the day for an easy *fast-food option* another teatime.' Sal, Cardiff

Cauliflower cheese

Serves 4 children

Suitable for ages 6 months +

❄ **Will freeze halfway through step 3, before cooking**

Nutrition ⬤ Fat ⬤ Saturates ◯ Sugar ◯ Salt

1 quantity cheese sauce (see page 134)

1 medium cauliflower

extra Cheddar cheese, for grating

NUTRITION NOTES

Rich in protein, calcium, vitamin C, fibre – a highly nutritious tea, and ideal for kids who need to put on a few pounds!

SERVING SUGGESTION

A light tea on its own but great with crusty bread and a side salad.

TIP

A quick and easy cauliflower cheese can be made just by pouring the cheese sauce over the cooked cauli florets, grating cheese over the top and flashing under the grill.

1 Preheat the oven to 180°C/350°F/Gas 4.

2 Make the cheese sauce if you haven't already. If necessary, warm it so that it pours easily – you can do this easily on medium in a microwave, in a microwaveable jug.

3 Cut the cauliflower into florets and put into a saucepan with a small amount of boiling water so that the florets aren't completely immersed – this will save more vitamin C. Parboil for around 6 minutes or until the florets are two-thirds cooked, then drain.

4 Arrange the florets in a gratin (ovenproof shallow) dish and pour over the cheese sauce to coat everything thoroughly. Sprinkle on the grated cheese and cook in the preheated oven for 20 minutes or until the cheese is golden and the sauce bubbling.

Variations

You can add all kinds of extras to cauliflower cheese to make it more substantial or for a change:

Netmums member Sally from Watford suggests adding cooked potato chunks or pre-cooked sausage chunks or bacon pieces.

Use half and half broccoli and cauliflower.

Scatter chopped firm fresh tomato amongst the cauliflower florets before you pour over the sauce.

Mini meatballs in tomato sauce

Meatballs are possibly the modern mums' home-made burgers. And, just like burgers, they are almost endlessly variable. Here we give you the classic recipe for meatballs made with beef.

450g good-quality minced beef

1 medium egg

2 tbsp finely grated Parmesan or
  mature Cheddar

1 large garlic clove, peeled, well
  crushed or chopped

1 tsp dried oregano

3 tbsp fresh white breadcrumbs

$\frac{1}{2}$ tsp freshly ground black pepper

a pinch of salt

1–2 tbsp olive oil

TO SERVE

1 quantity quick tomato sauce
  (see page 76)

NUTRITION NOTES
Good source of iron, protein, B vitamins
and beta-carotene.

SERVING SUGGESTION
Meatballs in tomato sauce are usually
served with spaghetti and a side salad,
but there is no reason why you can't
serve them with mashed potato or rice
and vegetables such as green beans or
broccoli.

TIP
If you have an electric food processor
you can whiz the ingredients up in that.

Serves 4 children

Suitable for ages 9 months +

✳ **Will freeze in a lidded container as a complete dish**

Nutrition   ⬭ Fat   ⬭ Saturates   ⬭ Sugar   ⬭ Salt

1   Combine all the meatball ingredients except the olive oil in a mixing bowl, using your hands. Roll around 30 mini balls from the mixture, laying them out on a plate as you do so.

2   Wash your hands thoroughly and heat the oil in a large non-stick frying pan over a medium high heat. Tip in the meatballs and fry, turning once or twice, until they are browned, which will take about 4–5 minutes.

3   Tip the tomato sauce into the pan, stir and bring to a simmer. Cook for 10 minutes and serve.

Variations

See below. Also, you can finely chop a couple of shallots or spring onions and add to the mix. You can omit the cheese (but it helps the meatballs remain moist). Similarly some people don't use breadcrumbs but often children prefer them with crumbs as they are softer. If you haven't time to make your own tomato sauce you can, of course, use ready-made good quality pasta tomato sauce or just some passata thickened with some red pesto.

You can use all kinds of meat with different flavourings. Try:

• Minced lamb with chopped fresh mint and rosemary •
Minced chicken with chopped parsley and thyme • Minced
pork with chopped sage and oregano • Minced beef or lamb
with ground cumin and/or coriander seeds • Vegetarian balls
can be made with the veggie burger mix (see page 87–8).

Fishcakes

'Fishcakes are such a lovely comfort food – you never grow out of loving the satisfied, warm, fulfilled feeling you get after a plate of home-made fishcakes. I'm sure this is why they are back on the menu at most top five-star restaurants. I hope my children order fishcakes in a restaurant in years to come and get a warm glow as they remember their childhood teas.'
Maria, mum to Stephen, Daniel and Rebecca

Serves 4–6 children

Suitable for ages 6 months +

※ **You can freeze the fishcakes after step 4, if the fish hasn't been previously frozen**

Nutrition   Fat   Saturates   Sugar   Salt

450g white fish fillets (haddock, coley, rock salmon or cod)

450g old potatoes

2 tbsp semi-skimmed milk

1 large egg or 2 small eggs, beaten

1–2 tbsp finely chopped parsley (optional)

4 slices stale white bread, crusts removed, made into breadcrumbs, or 100g ready-made crumbs from your freezer

a little plain flour

1–2 tbsp light olive oil

1 Poach the fish fillets in a pan of gently simmering water for a few minutes until just cooked, about 5 minutes. Don't overcook as the fish will continue to cook when you fry the fishcakes. Flake the fish and go over it for bones.

2 Meanwhile, peel the potatoes, cut into chunks and boil until a knife goes easily through them. Drain immediately, put the pan back on the hot hob for a few seconds, and shake to steam off any surplus water. You want the potatoes nice and dry so they don't make floppy, soggy fishcakes.

3 Mash the potato in the pan with the milk and the flaked fish, and add half the egg to bind. Add the chopped parsley at this point, if you're using it.

4 Spread the crumbs out on a large plate. Now flour your hands, and shape eight cakes from the mixture. Brush with a little of the beaten egg and then dip each side of each cake into the breadcrumbs to coat thoroughly. At this point you can put the cakes, covered, in the fridge until you are ready to cook.

5 Heat a large non-stick frying pan with 1 tbsp or so of oil and, when it is hot, add the cakes. You will probably need to do this in two batches or use two pans. Fry over a medium high heat until golden, about 4 minutes, then turn them over and fry the other side. Drain on kitchen paper and serve.

Continued

NUTRITION NOTES

White fish is a good source of protein, selenium and potassium while salmon is rich in omega-3s, which many kids don't get enough of in their diets, so do try the fishcakes with some salmon in them. Note that canned tuna doesn't count as an oily fish as it loses its omega-3 oils in the canning process. Orange sweet potatoes are a great source of carotenes, vitamins E and C.

SERVING SUGGESTION

Good with peas, green beans or broccoli and perhaps some tomato halves, lightly heated through in the fishcake frying pan.

Variations

Parsley does give a nice look and taste to the cakes but you can omit it if you like. Older children may enjoy the cakes made with finely chopped mild (jalapeño type) red seeded chillies or fresh coriander leaves instead of the parsley. An unusual change is to make the cakes with half ordinary potato and half orange-fleshed sweet potato.

You can use other types of fish. Salmon (or half salmon, half white fish) is very nice and looks pretty. Fresh tuna is another option (or, again, half and half), and if you're in a hurry or haven't any fresh fish or thawed frozen fish, you can use cans of tuna or salmon (preferably canned in water, as brine is too salty and oil will make the cakes rather oily).

If you are really pressed for time, you can actually omit the last part of step 4 and just shape the cakes then fry them as they are. As long as the cakes are not too soggy they work very well.

If you happen to have the oven on, you can bake the fishcakes on a non-stick baking tray for around 15 minutes at 180°C/350°F/Gas 4 or until lightly golden, turning them over halfway through. Brush them with a little light oil before baking to help the browning and to avoid sticking.

Netmums member Cathy says: 'Use small shaped cookie cutters to cut out shaped fishcakes. I serve fish shapes with sliced runner beans (seaweed) on blue plastic plates (sea). It doesn't really matter what shapes you use – the sea analogy has proved popular with lots of children, but rabbits have proved popular with my daughter, using beans as grass. Keep the shapes small, because then small people find them easy to pick up and eat.'

Netmums member Tracey says: 'I usually serve with peas and cherry tomatoes. My kids love them, and I love mine with sweet chilli sauce over the top while the kids have ketchup. Mmmmm.'

Bubble and squeak

This simple potato and vegetable side dish is one of the 'greats' in the family kitchen. We're not sure what happens to the greens in the process but they become totally delicious – even sprouts! Most kids love bubble and squeak even if they hate normal vegetables.

Serves 6–8 children (450g total weight of mix will make 6–8 small patties)

Suitable for ages 6 months +

❊ **The bubble and squeak will freeze after step 2**

Nutrition   ⬭ Fat   ⬭ Saturates   ⬭ Sugar   ⬭ Salt

---

cooked potato, mashed smoothly

about half the potato amount of cooked finely chopped cabbage or other green veg (see Variations)

salt and pepper (optional)

freshly grated nutmeg (optional)

a bit of butter or oil

NUTRITION NOTES

The squeak will probably end up with some vitamin C in it, and a good amount of fibre, but it does depend on what you put in. The saturate content will depend on whether you use butter or oil for frying.

SERVING SUGGESTION

Netmums member Helen from Poole, who sent in the recipe, says: 'Serve with a couple of slices of cold meat (ham or corned beef) and a dollop of tomato ketchup for a very quick, tasty meal.'

1 Mix the potato with the cabbage in a bowl until it is thoroughly combined. Add seasoning and a pinch of nutmeg if you want to use it.

2 Heat some butter or oil in a frying pan and add the mixture. You can either press it down into one 'cake' in the frying pan, or you can make small patties out of the mixture. Cook for 10 minutes, turning halfway through, or until the bubble and squeak is nicely browned on both sides.

Variations

You can use any type of cabbage, sprouts, broccoli or spinach. In fact you could add virtually any cooked veg, e.g. carrots, peas, peppers, but it wouldn't then be a traditional bubble and squeak!

Corned beef hash browns

There are hundreds of different versions of potato hash/hash browns/ vegetable hash around. The posh ones have you grate peeled potatoes and onion and mix them together before frying until golden. Most of us are probably too busy to grate a family-sized pile of potatoes and onions, and cooking these hash browns until the vegetables are actually no longer raw takes longer than you might imagine. You could parboil the potatoes and then grate them but they often break up in your hands while you attempt this feat. Here is an easier version of hash.

Serves 4 children

Suitable for ages 1 year +

❄ **Will freeze (best frozen before cooking)**

Nutrition ⬭ Fat   ⬭ Saturates   ⬭ Sugar   ⬭ Salt

350g old potatoes

1 small to medium mild onion

100g corned beef, chopped

2 tbsp light olive oil

NUTRITION NOTES
Corned beef is high in salt – at around 2g per 100g so this is a good way of serving it in small portions. Potatoes and onions are a reasonably good source of vitamin C.

SERVING SUGGESTION
Lovely with baked beans.

1   Peel the potatoes, cut into chunks and boil until just tender. Drain and tip into a bowl.

2   Peel and finely chop the onion. Stir the onions, corned beef and half the olive oil in with the potatoes.

3   Combine the mixture well until the potato is quite broken down, then form into rough patties.

4   Fry in the remaining olive oil in a pan over a medium to high heat for 5 minutes, turning once, until golden.

Variations

You can omit the corned beef for plain potato hash cakes.

You can add chopped chives or parsley to this mix or even use leftover fried onion.

You can use chopped spring onions or shallots instead of the medium onion.

You can also brush the cakes with oil and bake them in the oven at around 190°C/375°F/Gas 5 for 15–20 minutes instead of frying them – useful if you are serving a baked dish like cowboy chicken or chicken nuggets (see pages 121 and 48–9).

Firmer veg choices – chopped onions, carrots, broccoli, courgette, baby corn. Softer veg choices – mushrooms, fresh tomatoes, ready cooked (leftover) diced vegetables, defrosted frozen peas or small broad beans.

A tasty free-form vegetable hash sent in by Monica from Exeter. 'Peel and slice several potatoes and boil for about 8 minutes, then drain well. Heat a couple of tbsp olive oil in a frying pan. Add the potato (roughly crush if you like) and any firmer uncooked diced vegetables of your choice (see Variations), and cook on a medium-high heat for 8 minutes or until the potatoes are golden. Add sliced mushrooms or other soft vegetables (see Variations) and chopped garlic (optional), and cook for another 3 minutes. Add some canned, drained chopped tomatoes and cook for another 5 minutes. Add a dash of Worcestershire sauce and pepper and serve as a side dish or, if you sprinkle over grated cheese or stir in some cooked chicken or ham, you have a main meal.'

Stir-fries

'I used to think stir-fries were too grown up and a bit healthy-looking for my young children until we went to tea at a friend's and they demolished bowls of sweet prawns and little chicken pieces mixed in a gorgeous concoction of healthy-looking stuff. I asked my friend for a step-by-step guide and now I can toss together a healthy satisfying stir-fry in minutes. You just need the basics and a rough guide of what goes with what and you'll never look back. It's even replaced pasta as my fall-back meal.' Maxine, mum to Joseph, Alex, Isabelle and Lily

How did mums in the 1970s rustle up quick, tasty stove-top meals that everyone loves before we heard of stir-fries? Infinitely variable and always easy and quick, they've become one of our favourite modern standbys. And not least because you can always find one or two variations that even the fussiest kid will enjoy.

Basic stir-fry organisation and method

1   Collect and prepare all your ingredients. If not using ready-chopped meat/fish/veg etc., you need to make sure all this is done before you begin cooking – there won't be time during! Make sure all veggies are sliced to approximately the same size so that they take similar amounts of time to cook.

2   Cook your rice/noodles, drain and keep warm before you start the stir-fry. While the rice/noodles are cooking, do steps 3 and 4.

3   Make sure you have your cooking utensils, serving spoons and warm plates to hand and that the table's laid, including mats, accompanying sauces and drinks. If you are putting serving dishes on the table for children to help themselves, you might like to heat the oven and add the empty dishes so that they are warm when you add the stir-fry. Stir-fried foods quickly go cold.

4   Lay all the stir-fry ingredients out, preferably in the order things are going to go in the pan. This saves panicking when everything's sizzling.

With most stir-fries the ingredients will be:

Uncooked proteins: red meat, poultry, fish, tofu, Quorn. Listed here from longest to shortest cooking time.

Raw vegetables: peppers, broccoli, carrot, corn, green beans, onions, mushrooms, beansprouts. Listed here from longest to shortest cooking time.

Spices: e.g. chopped chilli, garlic, ginger.

Ready-cooked proteins: e.g. cooked chicken, meat, prawns.

Liquid sauces and flavourings.

Herbs and garnishes.

5   Heat 1–2 tbsp of light olive oil in a frying pan or wok. Later in the stir-fry process you can add a dash or two of a more highly flavoured oil to enhance the dish, e.g. sesame oil.

6   When the oil is nice and hot, add any uncooked meat/fish/tofu/Quorn, etc., preferably marinated. Stir-fry over high heat for a couple of minutes or until cooked through.

7   Remove the cooked protein to a warm plate near the hob, add a little more oil to the pan if necessary, or a dash of different oil, and add your vegetables, starting with those that take longest to cook. Stir all the time, and every minute or two add the next veggies to the pan until you add the softest ones, e.g. beansprouts or mushrooms, along with the spices.

8   Add your cooked proteins to the pan, either those that you have just cooked and reserved, or leftover cooked meats, etc., along with your sauce/liquid seasonings and stir for a minute or two, then finally, when all is cooked, garnish and serve.

TIP

If not marinated in your chosen sauce, then shake a little light soy sauce into the pan to colour the protein.

Your stir-fry sauce

You can of course use a ready-made sauce as there are some very good ones around. They tend to be high in sodium, though, and check the labels for monosodium glutamate to which some children react badly.

You can simply thin down a ready jar of sauce (e.g. yellow bean, black bean, hoisin, oyster sauce) with some gravy or stock you have in the fridge (light stock for yellow bean, dark for black bean) and add other flavourings, e.g. minced garlic or ginger.

You can make a fairly dry stir-fry; follow the stir-fry method and just add a dash of soy sauce and sesame or groundnut oil.

Or you can make your own more or less from scratch. Here are three ideas that you can whip up in a couple of minutes from storecupboard and fridge ingredients. All will make enough for a stir-fry for three to four children.
The cornflour, which is often included, is your thickener. When your mix goes into the pan, it will immediately bring the sauce together.

- *Chow mein/chop suey sauce for prawns/chicken/turkey/beef.* Combine 2–3 tbsp vegetable or chicken stock, 2 tbsp light soy sauce and 2 tsp cornflour.

- *Orange, honey and ginger sauce for chicken/pork.* Combine 2 tbsp orange juice, 1 tbsp stock, 2 tbsp light soy sauce, 2 tsp runny honey, 1 tsp minced ginger, 1 tsp minced garlic and 2 tsp cornflour.

- *Sweet and sour sauce for prawns/ chicken/pork.* Combine 75ml pineapple juice, 100g pineapple pieces (from can), 25ml tomato ketchup, 1 tbsp each wine vinegar and balsamic vinegar, 2 tbsp light soy sauce, 25ml rich chicken stock, 1 tsp honey and 2 heaped tsp cornflour.

TIP

Not all children like ginger, but most of the other flavours seem very acceptable to most kids; they often enjoy much stronger flavours than you would think.

Stir-fry variations

Not all stir-fries have to have an oriental flavour. You can stir-fry Mediterranean vegetables and add a tomato sauce; or use a mild curry sauce (e.g. masala) with suitable veggies such as broccoli, cauliflower and peas.

Listed here are ideas for foods that combine well with others in a stir-fry. This list is only a rough guide. By and large you can use what meat and vegetables you have; you will rarely find flavours that clash so much that you can't eat them with relish! But it is best to stick with one – or at most two – specialist sauce types. Soy sauce can be added to most dishes except sweet and sour.

Protein	Vegetables	Liquids, etc.	Spices/herbs
chicken	carrot, sweetcorn	orange, lemon	green chilli
turkey	broccoli	sweet chilli sauce	coriander leaves
pork, beef	sweet peppers onion, cabbage	black bean sauce oyster sauce	ginger, red chilli
prawns	mangetout, spring onions	sweet and sour	garlic, red chilli
tofu, Quorn	beansprouts	lemon, lime	

Simple chicken and vegetable stir-fry

Netmums member Yasmin from Liverpool: '*Stir-fries are a godsend in our house. I have the fussiest children in the world but for some reason they seem to happily tuck into stir-fries. I always get them to join in with the veg chopping so maybe they've worked up more of an appetite. Who knows!'*

Serves 3–4 children

Suitable for ages 5 years +

✳ **Will freeze**

Nutrition   ⬭ Fat   ⬭ Saturates   ⬭ Sugar   ⬭ Salt

---

3 chicken breast fillets (about 350g in all), cut into strips

1 tbsp groundnut or olive oil

100g broccoli florets

100g carrot, cut into strips

6 spring onions, finely chopped

1 garlic clove, well crushed

1 quantity chow mein sauce (see page 60)

NUTRITION NOTES

This is a good dish for getting children who are shy of vegetables to enjoy them, there is so much flavour and colour. Soy sauce is very high in salt, so always choose the light soy and use it sparingly. Make sure that the rest of the meal/day's eating is low in salt.

SERVING SUGGESTION

Serve combined with noodles for a chow mein, or on a bed of rice (which, if you like, you can stir with some fresh beansprouts for crunch) for chop suey.

1   Heat the oil in a large non-stick pan or wok. Over a high heat, stir-fry the chicken strips until they are golden and cooked through, about 4 minutes. Remove to a warm plate.

2   Add the vegetables (and a little extra oil if necessary) and stir-fry for a few more minutes until just tender. Add the garlic and stir for a minute, and then return the chicken to the pan.

3   Pour in the well-combined sauce and stir for a minute until it has thickened.

Variations

Endless! See Box (page 61) for inspiration.

Rice

'I used to be really wary of cooking rice as it so often stuck or went soggy but then someone told me the basics: 2:1 ratio of water to rice for 20 minutes, with the lid on. Now, I use rice for loads of things and the most popular is when I serve it in recycled takeaway containers: we have Chinese night (egg-fried rice), Indian night (with lightly spiced chicken and a pack of warmed poppadums). Another revelation is that cooked rice freezes brilliantly and only takes 2 minutes to defrost and heat up so I freeze it in takeaway cartons too.' Nikki, mum to Thomas and Madeleine

Rice is a healthy, low-fat carbohydrate and there are enough different varieties available to ensure that you can ring the changes. Most children really enjoy rice meals as they're so easy to eat and much less boring than meat and two veg!

Types of rice

Long-grain rice This is normal white rice used for many savoury dishes, as a rice side dish. Can be American or basmati (a tasty type from India). Quick-cook/easy-cook types have been partially cooked and cook in around 10 minutes. Normal white rice can take up to 20 minutes. Sachets of ready-cooked white rice make an easy (but expensive) side dish – just heat for a couple of minutes.

Brown rice This is long-grain rice before the outer husk has been removed. It contains more fibre and B vitamins than white rice and has a nutty flavour. It can take up to 40 minutes to cook, but quicker-cook varieties are available which may cook in around 20 minutes.

Risotto rice This special rice becomes creamy when cooked with liquids and makes it ideal for risottos. It can also be used for paellas. Arborio is the most easily found type.

Red and other coloured rices These can make a nice change from white rice and have similar nutrients.

Wild rice Isn't actually a rice, but a grass – its long black grains are quite hard and most kids don't enjoy them.

Basic rice

People tend to get in a panic over cooking rice, but if the rice is good quality (e.g. basmati) it is hard to ruin it. Just put water and rice in the pan in a ratio of 2:1, stir in a little salt, put the lid on and simmer very gently for 20 minutes for white, adding a little extra hot water if needed. Turn off the heat and leave for another couple of minutes, then fluff up gently with a fork. Don't cook rice in loads of water so that you have to drain it. You lose half the flavour that way and can end up with a soggy mess. For brown rice this method also works but follow the cooking time instructions on the pack as brands vary.

Variations on basic rice

Cook the rice in vegetable stock rather than water for extra flavour and a little colour.

Use saffron water for a lovely yellow rice (a sachet of saffron soaked in a little water for 15 minutes then added to the cooking water). A spot of turmeric is much cheaper but not all kids like the taste.

Stir in a few ground spices such as cinnamon – avoid whole spices as kids don't like them and you will have a job removing them before you serve.

Stir in some cooked petits pois and/or chopped herbs such as parsley before serving.

Netmums member Michelle from Bristol calls her variation 'Rice'n' Easy'. She waits until her rice is nearly cooked then adds cooked frozen peas, allows it to cool a little then adds chopped tomato, cucumber and ham. 'It always works!' she says.

Egg-fried rice

800g (about 4 servings) cooked
  long-grain white rice

2 medium eggs

1 dsp sesame oil (see Variations)

a little salt (optional)

1–2 tbsp groundnut oil (see
  Variations)

4 spring onions, finely chopped

NUTRITION NOTES

For young children, make sure the egg is thoroughly cooked with no raw bits left. White rice is a good source of energy for picky eaters but doesn't contain much in the way of vitamins or minerals. The egg adds several of these, including iron.

SERVING SUGGESTION

Lovely with any Chinese stir-fry or ribs, and is also tasty served cold as part of a buffet or with cold meats etc.

Serves 3–4 children

Suitable for ages 1 year +

✳ **Will freeze**

Nutrition   ⬭ Fat   ⬭ Saturates   ⬭ Sugar   ⬭ Salt

1 In a bowl, lightly beat the eggs with the sesame oil and a little salt if using.

2 Heat the groundnut oil in a wok or large non-stick frying pan and add the cooked rice, stirring for a few minutes until it is thoroughly hot.

3 Add the egg mixture, drizzling it all around the pan, and stir for another few minutes until the egg is cooked through, then stir in the onions just before serving.

Variations

You can omit the onions and use petits pois instead. You can stir in some small cooked prawns or little pieces of chicken or pork. Use light olive oil if you don't have groundnut and sesame oil in the cupboard.

Kedgeree

Netmums member Kelly from Swansea: *'This is one of my standard dishes that I wheel out once or twice a month. I often do it when the children have friends coming round and I serve it up in nice little dishes so they don't feel overwhelmed with a huge quantity.'*

Serves 4 children

Suitable for ages 1 year +

Nutrition Fat   Saturates   Sugar   Salt

400g undyed smoked haddock

3 lemon slices (optional)

300ml milk

60g butter

1 medium onion, finely chopped

2 tsp paprika (optional)

200g long-grain rice

1 litre chicken stock

3 hard-boiled eggs, peeled and
   roughly chopped

NUTRITION NOTES
Always choose undyed smoked haddock – the bright yellow dyed haddock contains colourings to which children may react badly. Haddock is a good source of protein and the eggs add more protein as well as B vitamins, zinc, iron and a host of other goodies.

SERVING SUGGESTION
Kedgeree is very nice served with mango chutney, as a brunch, lunch or supper dish, and is ideal for parties too.

1   Put the smoked haddock in a deep frying pan with the lemon (if using, it adds flavour), cover with milk and simmer for 6 minutes, or until cooked through. Remove the fish with a slotted spatula and flake, taking care to remove any bones.

2   Melt the butter in a lidded frying pan, add the onion and cook for 5 minutes then add the paprika (if using), and cook for another 2 minutes. Add the rice and stir to coat in the oil.

3   Now pour in the chicken stock, bring to the boil, put a lid on and simmer until the stock is absorbed and the rice is cooked. The length of time depends on the rice you're using so you may need to add more water to stop it boiling dry before the rice is cooked.

4   Add the fish and eggs and mix in carefully.

Variations
You can use vegetable or fish stock or even water. You can cook the haddock in water and use the water as part of the stock. You can add cooked peas and/or finely chopped fresh parsley to make the dish prettier and increase the vitamin C/fibre content. You can use mild curry powder instead of the paprika.

Basic risotto

Most children love this because it is so creamy. Risotto is quite easy despite what you may have heard. If you're really pushed for time you can actually miss out all the stirring of step 3, put the rice and all the stock in a lidded ovenproof dish and cook it in the oven at 170°C/325°F/Gas 3 for 30 minutes or so, stirring halfway through – check near the end of the time to make sure it doesn't need any more stock adding.

Serves 3–4 children as a side dish, 2–3 as a main

Suitable for ages 6 months +

Nutrition   ⬤ Fat   ⬤ Saturates   ⬤ Sugar   ⬤ Salt

1 tbsp olive oil

1 medium onion, finely chopped

300g risotto rice (e.g. arborio)

900ml vegetable or chicken stock, hot

1 Heat the oil in a large pan and sauté the onion over a medium heat, stirring now and then, until it is transparent and just softened – this will take a few minutes.

2 Add the rice and stir well to coat all the grains, then cook, stirring, for another minute or two.

3 Now add a quarter of the hot stock (from another pan – preferably one with a pouring lip on it – on a low hob so that it keeps hot), stir and bring to a simmer. Stir while the rice absorbs the liquid and then add another quarter, repeat the process and continue until all the stock is used up and the rice is tender and creamy. This will take about 20–25 minutes. Test the rice by eating a forkful, to make sure it is tender. If you run out of stock, just add hot water until the rice is cooked. But towards the end of cooking time don't add too much liquid at once as you don't want the risotto over-runny.

NUTRITION NOTES

Risotto rice isn't very high in nutrients but when your bits and pieces are added it can be a good way of getting the kids to eat vegetables.

SERVING SUGGESTION

Always nice with a bowlful of grated cheese handed round. Good as a supper on its own or the basic risotto can be a side dish.

Variations

- You can use half and half butter and oil for a richer flavour (but more saturates!). At its most basic you can just add some grated Cheddar and/or Parmesan cheese and stir in before serving. You can also add a little cream if you like, and salt or pepper (but remember if you've used stock cubes, they are salty).

- Cooked frozen mixed vegetables or peas and cubes of ham stirred in a few minutes before end of cooking to warm through thoroughly.

- 1–3 cloves well-crushed garlic added at end of onion cooking time and a little lemon juice added when the risotto is nearly ready.

- Strips of cooked chicken or turkey added towards the end of cooking time.

- Add 200g chopped chestnut mushrooms at step 2 and finish with chopped parsley for easy mushroom risotto, or add chopped tomatoes halfway through step 3 for tomato risotto.

- Chopped unsmoked bacon can be added with the onion. Nice with the mushrooms as well.

Pasta

'What would we do without pasta in our house?! We know we are going to have it at least three times a week. It's quick, easy, and I know the kids will eat it. My problem is I only know how to do three types of sauces or toppings that I just rotate. I know there are hundreds of other things I could be doing with pasta. Can you help me make it a bit more interesting?' Linda, mum to Steven, Luis and Harry

Pasta is perhaps the most-loved of all foods by children everywhere – easy and fun to eat and endlessly adaptable and variable. It is also a mum's blessing as it is low-cost, healthy, quick and simple. Here we look at all the ways you can use pasta to make fabulous child-friendly teas on the hob. (For Pasta Bakes, see page 125.)

A bit about pasta

Dried pasta is usually just a mix of hard wheat (durum is best) and water. Fresh pasta often contains eggs as well – and cooks more quickly.

You can of course make your own pasta but most busy mums wouldn't consider this as there is so much good pasta, both fresh and dried, to be bought cheaply.

Most pasta sold is white pasta, made from white flour. This means that it contains little fibre and few B vitamins and other trace nutrients but is a good source of calciuim and energy. Coloured pasta (e.g. tricolour) contains tomato in the red shapes and spinach in the green shapes. The nutrient content of these is similar to white. Wholewheat pasta is high in fibre, B vitamins, magnesium and iron so is a really good food for children and teens. But it hasn't, to many minds, got such a good texture as good-quality white and it takes longer to cook, around 20 minutes, to white pasta's 10 minutes. A good compromise is semi-wholewheat.

There are conflicting views about including oil when cooking pasta but, as a rule of thumb, adding a dash to the boiling water will help to prevent poor quality pasta from sticking.

Different pasta shapes

Traditionally in Italy different shapes are used with different types of sauce. Here is a brief guide to the most popular shapes on sale and what you might use them with – but really, it is up to you and what you have in your larder!

Quills (penne), rigatoni and macaroni These tubes are ideal for thick and hearty sauces.

Shells (conchiglie) and bows (farfalle) Great for chunky sauces.

Spirals (fusilli) Hold plenty of sauce as there is so much surface.

Tagliatelle These flat long strips are traditional with carbonara-type and fine-textured sauces.

Spaghetti The pasta most often used with bolognese, seafood and tomato sauces, but also great with thin sauces such as plain oil and garlic.

TIP

The smaller shapes are often less messy and easier for young children to eat. If serving long spaghetti you can always cut it up before serving.

Cooking pasta

Allow about 1 litre of water per 100g dry pasta. Bring the water to the boil, adding a little salt (optional, but it does bring out the flavour) and a dash of a light olive oil to stop the pasta sticking together. (If you're worried about adding oil, a dash will do no harm and most of it is thrown away with the water.) When the water is bubbling nicely, add the pasta and stir. If putting long spaghetti in the pan, wait a minute and you will find the pasta has softened enough to allow you to curl the pasta into the water. Bring back to the boil, don't cover, and keep a good boil throughout cooking time.

Follow the pack instructions for length of cooking time, but always check a piece of pasta before draining to make sure it really is cooked, as the times can only ever be a guide. Drain into a large colander. To keep warm if your sauce isn't ready, tip back into the cooking pan with 1–2 tbsp hot water, put on lid and replace on the turned-off hob, which will retain some heat.

TIP

Buy the best-quality durum wheat pasta you can, as cheap pastas tend to be harder to cook well and break up in the pan very quickly.

Top 4 Pasta Sauces for Children

You can probably make these sauces in less time than it would take to go to the shops and buy one – and they all taste great!

Bolognese sauce

Serves 4 children

Suitable for ages 9 months +

❄ **Will freeze in bags or lidded container**

Nutrition ⬭ Fat   ⬭ Saturates   ⬭ Sugar   ⬭ Salt

1 tbsp light olive oil

1 medium onion, finely chopped

1 large carrot, peeled and finely chopped

1 medium celery stalk, finely chopped

350g lean minced beef or lamb

200g canned chopped tomatoes

1 tbsp tomato purée

approx. 200ml beef or lamb stock

1 tsp dried mixed herbs

1 tsp Worcestershire sauce

NUTRITION NOTES

A great range of nutrients are in this filling sauce, and it's another superb way to get vegetables into children who don't normally like them. If you can find extra-lean minced beef, the saturated-fat content may go as low as Green.

SERVING SUGGESTION

Serve with short spaghetti/penne. Needs a green side salad and for hungry people, garlic bread goes down well!

1   Heat the oil in a large non-stick frying pan, and add the onion, carrot and celery. Sauté over a medium to high heat, stirring from time to time, until the onion and celery are transparent and soft, about 5 minutes.

2   Push the veg to the edge of the pan and add the meat, turn the heat up a bit and stir for a few minutes until it is browned. Stir in the tomatoes and tomato purée and mix everything together well, then add half the stock, the herbs and sauce, and stir again.

3   Bring to a simmer, turn the heat down, put a lid on and cook for at least 30 minutes, checking every 10 minutes or so, or until everything is cooked and you have a good rich-looking sauce. If during cooking the mix looks too dry, add some more of the stock.

Variations

You can add chopped mushrooms (towards the end of step 1), which contribute flavour and colour. You could even add chopped green or red peppers (at start of step 1). If using lamb, leek can be used instead of celery. You can omit the carrot without any great worries.

Easy carbonara sauce

Sent in by Netmums member Fran. *'I love this recipe because it is creamy and delicious but you don't have to waste time making a roux sauce. It's so easy and our kids really like it.'*

Serves 4 children

Suitable for ages 1 year +

Nutrition   ● Fat   ● Saturates   ○ Sugar   ◐ Salt

1 tbsp light olive oil

200g button mushrooms, sliced

8 rashers lean back bacon, sliced

1 tsp crushed garlic (optional)

75g mature Cheddar, grated

4 tbsp thickened or normal
  double cream

black pepper

NUTRITION NOTES

As this sauce is high in fat and saturates, and quite high in salt, it isn't one you want to serve the kids every day -- but on the plus side, it contains calcium, protein, B vitamins, and a lot of immune-boosting zinc.

SERVING SUGGESTION

This sauce is good with pasta spirals, penne or tagliatelle. Serve with a leafy salad and perhaps with some crusty bread.

TIP

When frying or grilling bacon, don't cook it until there are charred bits, as these are carcinogenic, i.e. they might increase the risk of cancer.

1   While your pasta is boiling, heat the oil in a non-stick frying pan and fry the mushrooms and bacon, adding the garlic for the last couple of minutes of cooking time if using. Have your other ingredients ready.

2   Once the pasta is cooked, drain well. Add the fried mushrooms and bacon to the pasta pot and then add the grated Cheddar, cream and lots of ground black pepper to taste. More or less cream can be added depending how light or creamy you want it to be.

Variations

You can use other types of cream if you have them to hand. You can use ham instead of bacon to save cooking it. You can add small cooked peas or sweetcorn kernels. You can omit the mushrooms but add sliced chicken breast (at step 1) instead. With this latter variation, you can add some ready-made red pesto to the creamy sauce for a delicious change.

Tomato and cheese sauce

Serves 4 children

Suitable for ages 6 months +

❄ **Will freeze**

Nutrition ▨ Fat   ▨ Saturates   ▨ Sugar   ▨ Salt

---

*1 quantity quick tomato sauce
(see page 76)*

1–2 tbsp thick single cream

75g mozzarella cheese, grated

*a handful of basil leaves
(optional), torn*

NUTRITION NOTES

High in vitamins E, C and carotenes, as
well as potassium and, in the cheese,
calcium, which also provides protein.

SERVING SUGGESTION

Serve with short spaghetti or spirals.
Needs only a green leaf side salad.

1   Heat the sauce up in a frying pan if using from fridge or
freezer. Add the cream and stir through thoroughly to warm.

2   Add the cheese, which will melt slightly, and the basil
leaves, and serve.

Variations

You can add drained canned tuna with the cream. You can
add slices of ham. You can omit the cream altogether. You
can add small chunks of cooked Mediterranean vegetables,
e.g. courgettes or peppers.

Double salmon sauce

Sent in by Gail from Suffolk.

Serves 4 children

Suitable for ages 5 years + (or 1 year + if you substitute the smoked salmon for more flaked salmon)

Nutrition   ⬤ Fat   ⬤ Saturates   ⬭ Sugar   ⬭ Salt

1 bunch spring onions, trimmed
  and chopped

about 10g unsalted butter

150g cooked salmon, flaked (see
  Variations)

100g smoked salmon

1 x 200g tub crème fraîche

1 tsp fresh chopped or freeze-dried
  dill (see Variations)

1 tbsp lemon juice

NUTRITION NOTES
This is a good way to get children to eat
some fish. While the fat content from
the crème fraîche is quite high, there
are also good omega fats here and a
good amount of protein.

SERVING SUGGESTION
Good with pasta bows or shells, and
mangetouts or broccoli.

1   While the pasta is cooking, soften the spring onions in the
    melted butter in a non-stick frying pan for a few minutes.
    Turn the heat off but leave the frying pan over the hob.

2   Add both types of salmon, the crème fraîche, dill and lemon
    juice. Mix well and leave to warm through until your pasta is
    ready.

Variations
You can buy ready-cooked, flaked salmon pieces in most
supermarkets, but you could also prepare your own – just
microwave 150g salmon fillet on high for 3 minutes or so,
then flake. Dill is traditional with salmon but some children
might not enjoy it – you could use chopped parsley instead.

CHEAT'S MACARONI CHEESE
Sent in by Netmums member, Annette. *'Nice and
easy and a real favourite with my family. It was
invented by my dad!'*

For a family of four, cook 250g macaroni.
Meanwhile, chop an onion and fry it in a little oil.
Empty a tin of chopped tomatoes and a tin of
baked beans into a shallow heatproof dish and
add the cooked macaroni and about 60g grated
Cheddar. Stir well, then microwave, covered, on
high for 4–5 minutes.

EASIEST EVER PASTA DISH!
This is a recipe from Lucy from Hillingdon, Sally
from Richmond and Sharon from Cardiff.

Cook your pasta (as page 69) and add broccoli
florets to the pan for the last 5 minutes of cooking
time (or steam it above the pasta if you have a
steamer). When it is all cooked, drain and stir in a
good tablespoon of cream cheese until it is
melted. Hey presto – pasta with vegetable and
cheese sauce! Also works well with frozen veg,
courgette pieces and you can add ham.

*'We love this because it saves on washing-up, as
you use just one pan!'*

Netmums member Cherie has a similar recipe, but
uses ready-made green pesto instead of the
cream cheese.

Pizzas

'My son told me after a play date that he loves going to Sam's house for tea as his mum makes pizza from scratch! He said this with such wide-eyed reverence that I set out to find out how. I wanted to be as good as "Sam's mum"! Home-made pizza is now one of my regular weekly suppers and is actually simple and quite relaxing to prepare. The children help with the toppings (often nibbling the raw vegetables such as red pepper as we go), and of course they love anything they are allowed to eat with their fingers (who did invent the knife and fork?!) I always try and invite one of their friends for tea (or Saturday lunch) on Pizza Day. Firstly because I know they'll like the food, and secondly I'm hoping they'll go home and tell their mum how great I am!' Jacqui, mum to Zachary and Reuben

Pizza is a perennial kiddies' favourite and if you have a few pizza bases in the freezer you're never stuck for a quick tea. Home-made pizza is tastier and more healthy than most bought ones so why not try our basic pizza recipe? Yes, making the pizza dough isn't that quick, but you can make up a batch on a wet weekend afternoon with the kids and freeze the bases ready for topping. Or you could make them up complete with topping and freeze – that's up to you! If you don't have time to do the dough from scratch and have none in the freezer, make the dough using a pizza dough mix (widely available in supermarkets), which is much nicer than the ready-made bases. The tomato sauce is another easy item to make (yes really!) and is best done in batches.

Netmums member Jenny says: 'The kids love it when I suggest pizza for supper – if I catch them on a good day, they get their aprons on and get stuck in with kneading the dough. Although I have to admit that now I've got a bread-maker I tend to by-pass that bit and get them to add the toppings instead.'

QUICK PIZZA CHEATS
- Use mini or full-size pitta breads (white works best), spread over the top with tomato sauce, cheese and topping and cook under a hot grill until bubbling.
- Use halved baguettes, bagels or English muffins in the same way – even better if you have time to lightly toast them before spreading on the topping.
- If you have no home-made tomato sauce, of course use a good ready-made one, or even just spread with tomato purée mixed half and half with Sacla red pesto (not for children with nut allergy) or, to keep things very simple, just use tomato purée.

Basic cheese and tomato pizza

Makes 1 x 30cm pizza to serve up to 4 children (if batch making, increase quantities accordingly)

Suitable for ages 1 year +

✳ Uncooked bases and cooked tomato sauce can be frozen separately or as finished pizza. Bag bases separately to freeze

Nutrition   ⬭ Fat   ⬭ Saturates   ⬭ Sugar   ⬭ Salt

DOUGH

225g strong white flour, plus extra for dusting

¼ tsp salt

½ tsp easy-blend yeast

150ml warm water

1 tbsp light olive oil

TOPPING

1 quantity quick tomato sauce (see page 76)

100g soft mozzarella cheese (ball type)

1 large tomato (or 2 medium), thinly sliced

2 tbsp freshly grated Parmesan (or mature Cheddar)

NUTRITION NOTES

High calcium and good amounts of vitamin C, carotene, and a wide range of other vitamins and minerals.

SERVING SUGGESTION

Garnish with fresh basil leaves; serve with a mixed leaf salad; potato wedges (see page 104). For hungry children after a busy day and for a main meal, many of them do want a few oven potatoes or similar with their pizza. The pizza and salad alone don't add up to a great deal of calories.

1   To make the dough, sift the flour and salt into a large mixing bowl and stir in the yeast. Make a well in the centre and pour in half the water and the oil. Mix with a fork, adding more of the water as necessary, until you have a soft dough.

2   Turn the dough on to a floured, dry, clean kitchen surface or large board and knead (the kids like doing this!) for about 10 minutes until the dough looks and feels smooth and elastic. Put it in an oiled bowl, cover and leave in a warm corner of the kitchen to rise for an hour by which time it should have doubled in size.

3   Meanwhile, make the tomato sauce and set aside to cool. Preheat the oven to 220ºC/425ºF/Gas 7.

4   When the dough is ready, put it back on the work surface and roll it out to around 30cm in diameter. Spread the tomato sauce over it, leaving 2cm round the edges.

5   Arrange the sliced mozzarella on top followed by the tomato slices and grated Parmesan. Now is the time to add any other toppings you like (check the Box below), followed by a last sprinkling of grated cheese.

6   Cook in the preheated oven for 20 minutes or until the topping is bubbling and golden, and the edges of the base are nicely light brown.

TOPPINGS
- Skinned cooked sliced chicken and sliced button mushrooms.
- Diced chorizo, salami, pepperoni, Parma ham (these are quite high in salt!) and thinly sliced red onion.
- Canned, well-drained fish, e.g. tuna, and halved cherry tomatoes.
- Cherry tomatoes (halved) and baby spinach leaves.
- Cooked sweetcorn kernels, pineapple pieces, diced ham.
- Roasted or stir-fried mixed Mediterranean vegetables (e.g. sliced courgette, aubergine, red onion, tomato, pepper).

Quick tomato sauce

Makes enough for 1 large pizza or 2–4 small pasta dishes

Suitable for ages 6 months +

❄ **Will freeze in lidded container or strong bag**

Nutrition ⬭ Fat ⬭ Saturates ⬭ Sugar ⬭ Salt

1 tbsp light olive oil

1 medium onion, peeled and finely chopped

1 medium garlic clove, peeled and crushed or chopped

1 x 400g can chopped tomatoes, or 4 medium whole tomatoes (350g)

1 rounded dsp sun-dried tomato paste or tomato purée

1 level tsp caster sugar

juice of ½ lemon

black pepper

a pinch of salt (optional for ages 1 year +)

1 Heat the oil in a lidded non-stick frying pan and stir-fry the onion over a medium heat for 5 minutes or until soft and transparent.

2 Add the garlic and stir for a minute, then add the rest of the ingredients. Stir well, bring to a simmer, cover and cook over a medium low heat for 20 minutes.

3 Take the lid off and simmer for another 10 minutes or so, until the sauce is nice and thick.

Variations

You can add chopped fresh or dried herbs (e.g. parsley, basil, thyme), but remember very young children may find some herbs (e.g. rosemary) too strong. For older kids add extra garlic or some fresh finely chopped mild jalapeño-type seeded chilli.

NUTRITION NOTES

Rich in carotene, good source of vitamins C and E and potassium.

SERVING SUGGESTION

Use on pizza or in recipe of your choice (ideal for pasta) or in other recipes in this book.

TIP

To skin a tomato, make a cross on the bottom with a sharp knife and then put in a bowl and cover with boiling water for a minute. Remove from the water and take off the skin. To seed, slice in half and use a teaspoon to get the seeds out. The point of this is to avoid the mix being too runny – a runny mix will give you a soggy base unless it is eaten immediately.

Eggy Things

'My children love being *allowed to break the eggs* into a bowl, and *(unless it's a recipe that calls for an unbroken yolk)* it's the one time that *breaking something* is actually the *aim of the activity!*' Jane, mum to Holly, Zach and Selene

'Chick Chick Chick Chick Chicken
Lay a little egg for me
Chick Chick Chick Chick Chicken
I want an egg for my tea
I haven't had an egg since breakfast and now it's half-past three, so
Chick Chick Chick Chick Chicken
    Lay a little egg for me.'

Eggs are perhaps the most perfect food for children. Low-cost, quick, easy and highly nutritious, they make a great meal, snack, lunchbox item or part of a meal or salad. Once children are over six months you can give them hard egg yolk; once over nine months they can have hard-cooked white as well. Up until around three years, they shouldn't be given runny parts of the egg at all, to avoid any chance of salmonella.

What type of egg?

Battery	Cheapest eggs, mass produced, may be termed 'farm fresh' or other meaningless phrases. The hen's feed can include artificial additives.
Lion eggs	A UK symbol with a salmonella-free guarantee, used on all types of eggs as an 'assurance' symbol.
Free range	The hens have more space, are free to roam around in large sheds and have access to daylight.
Organic	The hens lead a fairly natural life on outdoor organic ground and are fed no lower than 80% organic feed. The eggs may be higher in omega-3 fats.

Classic Spanish omelette

The Spanish omelette or tortilla is similar in concept to the Italian frittata. Call it what you like, it is very moreish and easy – less fraught than trying to produce a fluffy mound of French omelette! There is also less chance of serving up runny egg when it is cooked this way.

Serves 3–4 children

Suitable for ages 1 year +

Nutrition   ◖ Fat   ◖ Saturates   ◔ Sugar   ◌ Salt

400g old potatoes (waxy kind)

1 tbsp light olive oil

1 medium onion, peeled, halved and thinly sliced

6–8 eggs, depending on size

salt and pepper

NUTRITION NOTES

Great for iron, protein, vitamins A, B12, folate, D, C, potassium and more. Organic eggs may contain more of the important omega-3 fats, or you can buy specially produced eggs high in these oils. All eggs should be fresh, used before their use-by date, and throw them away if cracked.

SERVING SUGGESTION

Ideal with chunks of bread, sauté potatoes, mixed salad or peas. Cool, it makes a great lunchbox or picnic addition.

1 Peel the potatoes and cut into large chunks. Boil until just tender, drain and allow to cool a little.

2 Heat the oil in a non-stick frying pan with rounded edges and sauté the onion over a medium heat for 8–10 minutes or until it is completely soft and transparent, stirring from time to time. Meanwhile, beat the eggs in a bowl with a tbsp of water and a pinch each of salt and pepper.

3 When the onion is cooked, arrange the potato chunks evenly in the pan and then pour the egg mixture over evenly. Cook over a medium heat for a few minutes. Meanwhile heat the grill.

4 When the underside of the omelette is golden, move the pan under the grill (take care to have the handle outside the grill as it will get very hot otherwise), and cook the top of the omelette until it is golden too, and the egg is just cooked all the way through (leave it too long and it may turn out dry and rubbery). Turn the omelette out on to a plate, cut into wedges and serve hot or cold.

Variations

- This basic onion and potato omelette is the traditional Spanish recipe but you can add more or less what vegetables you feel like: cooked peas, sweetcorn or thinly sliced button mushrooms can be added to the pan with the potatoes, or uncooked thinly sliced/chopped veggies such as courgettes or red pepper can be added with the onion.

- You can also sprinkle chopped parsley or other herbs into the egg mix if your children like herbs, or grate cheese on top before step 4.

Continued

- Netmums member Sandra has this oven-baked variation on the Spanish omelette: 'I put the potato into a greased quiche dish along with all the other vegetables and pour over egg mix (to which I add a little milk) and oven bake at 180°C/350°F/Gas 4 for about 20–25 minutes. The kids love it and I can simply mash it up for the youngest – even Dad enjoys this!'

- You can make a flat omelette more like a pizza by cooking the basic Spanish omelette then, before flashing under the grill, spread some ready-made tomato sauce over the top, followed by your mushrooms or cooked peppers, ham, etc., then grated cheese.

Egg in toast

Netmums member Jane from Ealing: *'This one is so much fun – children love it!'*

Use a pastry cutter to cut out a shape in the middle of a slice of bread. Toast the bit from the middle. Heat a bit of butter in a frying pan on a medium heat and when it's melted and hot put the slice of bread with the hole into the pan and let it cook until it goes a little brown. Flip it over and break an egg into the hole in the middle. Cook for about 3–4 minutes then scoop it out carefully with a spatula and serve it with the toasted shape on the side to use instead of a traditional 'soldier'. Make sure the yolk is cooked through for babies and toddlers. Use any type of bread: it works just as well with soda bread and rye bread.

Scrambled egg variations

- Basic scrambled egg is easily made in a non-stick saucepan using 1–2 eggs, 1–2 tbsp milk and 2 tsp butter per child. You can either cook it quickly over high heat, using a wooden curved spatula and in effect 'stir-frying' until it is cooked (don't stop stirring or the bottom will burn, and take it off the heat straightaway or it will go very dry), or cook it slowly over a low heat (less chance of burning but takes quite a while!) Don't serve runny (undercooked) egg to young children.

- Jazz your egg up with any of the following: small pieces of cooked ham, salmon, smoked salmon, bacon, grated cheese, chopped tomato, chopped fresh parsley, cooked sweet peppers, chopped.

More eggy ideas

- Poached eggs (for children school age + if they are still runny) on mashed potato instead of toast.

- Poached eggs on a bed of steamed spinach, covered with cheese sauce.

- Poached eggs in a nest of cooked mixed sweet peppers, baked in the oven for 15 minutes or until cooked – older children love this.

- Leftover omelette strips stirred into cooked rice for added nutrition.

- Hard-boiled egg quarters with canned tuna, sliced tomato and finely chopped spring onions – serve with bread for a quick summer tea.

- For eggy bread, beat together some raw egg and milk with a dash of seasoning. Slice your loaf then dip in the egg mixture before frying in some butter/light oil mix until golden on both sides. You can add sugar and cinnamon to the egg for a sweet version.

Toppings

Toast! Baked potatoes! Children's favourite carbohydrates, and very handy they are too. But what to put on *top* of them to make a change from Marmite, jam, cheese or a can of beans? Here are a few of our ideas for some tasty but not too complicated toppings for toast and fillings for baked potatoes.

Welsh rarebit

You could just settle for cheese on toast ... or you could push the boat out and make this tasty alternative with its extra flavours and nutrients.

Serves 4 children

Suitable for ages 1 year +

Nutrition ● Fat ● Saturates ○ Sugar ○ Salt

1 small onion, peeled and finely chopped (optional)

2 tsp slightly salted butter

about 150g Cheddar cheese, grated, or enough to cover 4 slices bread

1 medium egg, beaten

1 tbsp Worcestershire sauce

4 slices bread

sweet chutney

1 Cook the onion gently in the butter for 5 minutes. Add the cheese, beaten egg and Worcestershire sauce and mix together as the cheese melts. Meanwhile toast the bread on one side.

2 Spread the untoasted side of the bread with chutney, then top with the cheese mixture. Cook it under a medium to hot grill until golden and puffy.

Variations

You can omit the onion and/or the chutney, or use tomato ketchup instead of the chutney. Try other cheeses or combinations of cheeses – e.g. mozzarella or Emmental.

NUTRITION NOTES

This is a high-fat meal with quite a lot of salt in it but it is also rich in nutrients important for children, such as calcium, iron and protein.

SERVING SUGGESTION

Serve on its own as a light supper, or with a selection of vegetables.

TASTY TOAST

Sent in by Vickie from Twickenham. *'Super quick and nutritious favourite teatime meal for my kids aged three and 14 months.*

'Toast two to three slices of wholemeal bread on one side. In the meantime, remove bones from a can of sardines, pilchards or mackerel fillets in tomato sauce. Mash and mix in 75g or so of tasty grated hard cheese (e.g. mature Cheddar or Emmental). Spread the mixture generously on the untoasted side of the bread then toast under the grill until the cheese is melted and the mixture turns golden. I serve this with cucumber sticks or sweetcorn.'

Cheesey ratatouille

Sent in by Kim from Wellingborough. *This is a quick microwave-cooked version of ratatouille.*

Serves 4 children

Suitable for ages 1 year +

❄ Will freeze in lidded container or strong bag/s

Nutrition ◗ Fat   ◗ Saturates   ◗ Sugar   ◗ Salt

1 large onion, peeled and finely
  chopped

2–3 mixed sweet peppers, seeded
  and diced

2 tbsp light olive oil

1 garlic clove, peeled and chopped

1 small courgette, trimmed and
  diced

3 tomatoes, chopped

$1/2$ tsp dried basil or a few fresh
  leaves

2 tbsp tomato purée

30g (or more to taste) Cheddar
  cheese, grated

a pinch of salt (optional)

black pepper

1 Combine the onion, peppers, oil and garlic in a large microwaveable bowl. Cover and cook on full power for 5–6 minutes, stirring once.

2 Stir the courgette into the pepper mixture, cover and cook on full power for 5–6 minutes until the vegetables are tender. Stir once or twice during cooking.

3 Add the tomatoes to the cooked vegetables with the basil, tomato purée and cheese. Mix well, cover and cook on full power for 2 minutes. Season to taste.

Variations
Use red onion instead of the white. Older children may enjoy some fresh seeded and finely chopped mild jalapeño type chilli added at step 1. Fresh coriander makes a nice herbal change.

NUTRITION NOTES
This is a very healthy supper. Many children who don't like 'greens', or boiled or steamed veg will happily eat this and it is full of vitamin C, carotenes, fibre and plenty more.

SERVING SUGGESTION
Lovely with baked potato but also makes a great tea with crusty French bread for dunking.

JAZZED-UP BAKED BEANS
Sent in by Esme from Nottingham. *'Fry some finely chopped onion – plus whatever other veg you think you can get away with, e.g. mushrooms – in a small amount of olive oil until soft. Grill some good-quality sausages or bacon, then chop up into small pieces. Add the meat to the onion pan, and throw in a can of low-salt/sugar baked beans.*

'Now for the magic bit – add a tsp of molasses (available from health-food shops) to make it taste sort of caramelly and comforting! Black pepper is nice added here too. Great with either baked potatoes or wholewheat toast.'

Summer suppers and outdoor eating

There are fewer things that make life easier for mums than feeding the children outside. So from late spring to early autumn, take advantage of every fine day. Food preparation should be easy and fun, and preparing to eat outdoors is rarely a chore and – actual barbecuing apart – there should be plenty that the kids can help with and plenty of raw veg to be snacked on.

This is also the nicest time for inviting neighbours, friends and children's friends to eat with you. This chapter includes favourite ideas for outdoor food for family picnics, everyday teas on the patio and simple feasts for all occasions – from all the things that cook on the barbie to a range of salads and finger foods. If the weather lets you down, just turn on the grill and eat in the kitchen instead – it will all still taste wonderful.

Burgers

'The poor burger got a raw deal from the fast-food industry. Why should it be the symbol for junk food? A good burger, home-made with decent ingredients, is fine food and I have to agree with the children that food eaten Viking style with your bare hands is a truly satisfying experience. Bring on the guilt-free burgers!'
Caroline, mum to Abbie and Maisy

Simple home-made burgers and chips

Netmums member Melanie says: 'Real burgers and wonderful home-made chips – a true alternative to junk food.'

Serves 4 children

Suitable for ages 1 year +

❋ The burgers will freeze at end of step 1, individually wrapped in clingfilm

Nutrition   ◖ Fat   ◖ Saturates   ◖ Sugar   ◖ Salt

1 medium dessert apple, peeled and grated

450g lean minced beef

CHIPS

500g ready-boiled potatoes

2 tbsp light olive or groundnut oil

NUTRITION NOTES

Lean beef is a great source of iron for children, as it is very easily absorbed. It's also high in B vitamins.

SERVING SUGGESTION

Serve with a bun and salad or with baked beans or broccoli. If you have no ready-cooked potatoes you could serve the burgers with potato wedges (see page 104).

1 For the burgers, mix the apple and minced beef together thoroughly in a bowl and then shape and firmly press into eight small or four large burgers, squeezing the mix together so the burgers don't fall apart during cooking.

2 Grill, barbecue or dry-fry in a non-stick frying or griddle pan (brushed with a little oil) for about 5 minutes on each side until cooked through. Check there is no pink in the middle before serving – larger burgers will take longer.

3 For the chips, slice the cooked potatoes into chip shapes or rounds. Heat the oil in a frying pan and shallow-fry over a high heat for 2–3 minutes a side until the chips are golden and crisp on the outside. Drain on kitchen paper to remove excess oil.

Variations

- Add in a tsp of Marmite, a dash of Worcestershire sauce, sautéed finely chopped onions, mixed herbs, fresh chopped parsley, a tbsp of mayonnaise, or a tsp of low-salt stock bouillon to add more flavours to your burgers.

- You can also bind the mix with an egg if you like to help it hold together better.

- To bulk the meat out further and to make the burgers slightly softer, you can add 4–5 tbsp (about 40g) fresh soft breadcrumbs to the mix.

- You can use any sort of mince for this recipe (lamb, turkey, pork, chicken). If you have a food processor you can even buy beef steaks and mince them yourselves which would make them leaner.

Veggie burgers

There are hundreds of different recipes for vegetarian burgers – containing variations of vegetables, beans, nuts, seeds, and a myriad of flavourings and additions. Our veggie burger recipe's main ingredient is beans, as they are high in protein and a sensible substitute for meat for vegetarian children. Also they are suitable for younger children as they don't contain nuts or seeds.

Serves 4 children

Suitable for ages 1 year +

❄ **Will freeze before cooking**

Nutrition   ⬤ Fat   ◯ Saturates   ◯ Sugar   ◯ Salt

3 tbsp light olive oil

1 medium onion, peeled and finely chopped

1 garlic clove, peeled and finely chopped

1–2 tsp mixed dried herbs

400g mixed soft cooked/canned beans (see Tip page 88)

1 tbsp tomato purée

1 tbsp light soy sauce

1 tbsp lemon juice

50g fresh breadcrumbs

Continued

NUTRITION NOTES

Great bundle of nutrients here — B and E vitamins, folate, calcium, potassium, magnesium and plenty of fibre.

SERVING SUGGESTION

Serve as burgers (previous page).

TIP

Which beans to use? A mix of chickpeas, butter beans and red kidney beans is particularly nice. You can also use any combination of lentils, black-eye beans and cannellini beans. You can buy ready mixed cans of beans in the supermarket which are fine. Drain well and rinse before using. The drained weight of a 400g can of beans is about 300g. If you're cooking your own dried beans, 100g dried beans gives about 250g cooked weight.

1 Heat half the oil in a non-stick frying pan and cook the onion for a few minutes to soften, then add the garlic, herbs and beans. Stir the beans around and mash them down into the pan with a fork or potato masher for a couple of minutes, so that they are roughly puréed.

2 Add the tomato purée, soy sauce, lemon juice and breadcrumbs and mix well, taking the pan off the heat. Allow to cool a little.

3 Divide the mixture into 4 large or 8 small burgers and shape into patties with your hands.

4 Now in the cleaned pan, heat the rest of the oil and fry the burgers over a medium high heat for 3 minutes or so per side, or grill or barbecue until golden.

Variations

You can add a variety of finely chopped vegetables to the pan with the onions, e.g. carrot, red pepper, celery and mushroom. Cook until tender. You can add spicy flavourings using, for example, ground cumin, coriander or chilli. You can add green or red pesto (about 1 tbsp), and for children over 5 without nut allergy you can add chopped mixed nuts, ground nuts, and/or seeds.

On the Barbie

'We use our barbecue almost every evening in summer. It's just so much easier: the kids help prepare and carry food and drinks outside, my husband always does the cooking bit (what is it with men and barbecues!), the kids always seem to eat loads, there are never any arguments about sitting still at the table, and we often use paper plates so we just tip everything into the brown bin afterwards so there's not even any washing up. What's not to like!' Zoe, mum to Shannon and Kacey

If you're thinking of cooking meat, fish or poultry on the barbie, one of the best ways to get a delicious result is to first marinate the meat. This adds flavour and helps to tenderise it. For each of the following marinades, all you do is combine all the ingredients in a non-metallic shallow bowl (e.g. glass or china), stir very well and then add your pieces of meat or fish, making sure they are well coated. Cover the dish, pop in the fridge and leave for at least 30 minutes. A few hours is even better, but don't leave for longer than that, though: for example, if you leave fish in a marinade for a day, you will find it starts to disintegrate in the marinade acids! When it is time to cook, just remove the meat from the marinade and put on the barbie. You can use the leftover marinade to baste during cooking (but don't ever use it as a sauce as it will contain raw meat juices).

You can use any of these marinades with the kebab recipes that appear below. If you have an electric blender you can whiz up these marinades in seconds. A marinade shouldn't be too thick – it should be similar to gravy. If you blend a marinade and it comes out too thick, thin it down with water or stock and mix in well.

Marinades for fish

- Juice of 1–2 limes, 1 tbsp olive oil, a peeled and crushed garlic clove, 1 tsp caster sugar and $1/2$ tsp ground ginger or dill (optional). Great with salmon steaks.

- Juice of 1 ripe lemon, 2 tbsp olive oil, 2 peeled, crushed and well-chopped garlic cloves, 1–2 finely chopped shallots, 1 tbsp chopped flat-leaf parsley (curly will do), black pepper and a pinch of salt. Good with any white fish.

Marinades for chicken

- 200ml natural yoghurt, 1 tbsp favourite curry paste and a peeled and crushed garlic clove. Sent in by Nita from Tower Hamlets.

- 50ml orange juice, 25ml lemon juice, 1–2 tsp Dijon mustard, 1–2 tsp Worcestershire sauce, 50ml groundnut or light olive oil, 2 garlic cloves, peeled, crushed and chopped, 1 tbsp chopped mixed fresh herbs (e.g. rosemary, oregano, parsley, thyme) or 2 tsp dried herbes de Provence, a little black pepper, and a pinch of salt (optional).

Marinades for red meat

- 25ml red wine vinegar, 25ml balsamic vinegar, 2 peeled, crushed and chopped garlic cloves, 60ml tomato ketchup and 1 tbsp Worcestershire sauce. Good for lamb and beef.

- 150ml apple or pineapple juice, 2 tbsp soy sauce, 1 tbsp caster sugar, 1 garlic clove, peeled and crushed and $1/2$ tsp ground ginger (optional). Good for pork.

All-purpose marinade

- 1 small onion, peeled and finely chopped, 1 tbsp light olive oil, 1 tbsp runny honey, 3 tbsp tomato ketchup, 2 tbsp light soy sauce and 1 tsp Dijon mustard. To make this sweet and sour, add 1 tbsp white wine vinegar.

Barbecue tips

- Make sure the BBQ coals are glowing rather than flaming before you add food to the griddle. To make sure larger pieces of meat (e.g. chicken quarters) are cooking all the way through, keep them at the edges of the barbie for most of the cooking time, bringing them to the centre to brown for the last few minutes.

- You should soak wooden kebab sticks in water for 30 minutes before using, to avoid burning them. Otherwise, you can buy sets of metal kebab skewers.

- Take the food off sticks before serving to young children and, for slightly older children, cut the pointed ends off the sticks.

- Using a sharp knife always check that meat is cooked all the way through before serving, to avoid food poisoning. This is most important with poultry and items made from minced meat.

- Wrap the ends of chicken drumsticks in foil to make them easier to eat.

- Keep raw meat out of the hot sun and well covered to avoid contamination by insects and possible food poisoning.

- Often marinade recipes include white or red wine or sherry. Although the alcohol will be cooked off, you might prefer to substitute the same amount of suitable stock, which works nearly as well.

Vegetable kebabs

You don't really need a proper recipe for these. Simply choose your vegetables: red onions, red and yellow peppers, courgettes, mushrooms, aubergines, tomatoes. About 650–750g in all for a family of four or perhaps six children.

TIP
If you don't have any skewers handy, just brush larger pieces of vegetables with the balsamic/olive oil mix and cook them loose on the barbecue. A hinged rack, widely available, will help to hold small items all together and means you can turn them all over at once and remove them from the BBQ all together.

1   Peel, wash, etc., as necessary then cut them into squares or chunks, and divide between four to six skewers.

2   Mix 1 tbsp balsamic vinegar and 3 tbsp olive oil together and season lightly. Brush this dressing over the vegetables.

3   Barbecue for 5 minutes, turning, until softened and charred.

Sausagemeat and bacon kebabs

450g pork (or beef) sausagemeat

1 tbsp BBQ seasoning

*75g unsmoked bacon, finely
  chopped*

*1 large yellow pepper, seeded and
  cut into 2.5cm squares (you need
  12 pieces in all)*

NUTRITION NOTES

Good for vitamin B group, but
sausagemeat is always quite high in fat
so serve with plain salad and some
good bread to keep the meal balanced.

Serves 4 children

Suitable for ages 2 years +

Nutrition ● Fat ● Saturates ○ Sugar ○ Salt

1   Thoroughly combine the sausagemeat, seasoning and
    bacon in a mixing bowl. Divide the mixture into 16 and roll
    into balls. Thread four balls on to each of four skewers,
    alternating with the squares of pepper.

2   Place on a medium hot barbecue or under a preheated grill
    for 10–15 minutes, turning occasionally, until cooked.

Variations
You could if you prefer leave the bacon out of the balls, cut it
into squares and thread on to the sticks with the balls and
peppers.

Lamb and tomato kebabs

*600g lean lamb (e.g. leg fillet or
  neck fillet)*

1 tbsp olive oil

juice of $1/2$ lemon

*1 good tsp dried mixed
  Mediterranean herbs*

*1 large garlic clove, peeled and
  well crushed*

$1/2$ tsp sweet paprika (optional)

8–12 small cherry tomatoes

*6 small sweet shallots, peeled and
  halved*

NUTRITION NOTES

Fantastic source of B vitamins, iron,
zinc and potassium.

Serves 4 children

Suitable for ages 2 years +

Nutrition ○ Fat ○ Saturates ○ Sugar ○ Salt

1   Cut the lamb into bite-sized cubes and put in a glass or
    china dish. Now in a small bowl, mix together the olive oil,
    lemon juice, herbs, garlic and paprika. Spoon over the lamb
    and stir well to coat all the meat. Leave for an hour or so if
    possible.

2   When ready to cook, heat the barbecue (or grill) to medium-
    high.

3   Add the tomatoes and shallots to the marinating meat and
    stir. Now thread everything alternately on to 4 kebab sticks
    and cook for around 10 minutes, turning a few times and
    basting with any marinade that remains in the dish (or with
    a little oil).

Variations

- You can use skinless chicken or lean beef or pork fillet instead of the lamb.
- You can use ready-crushed garlic from a jar to save time.
- You can use squares of green pepper instead of the onion, or omit and add extra tomatoes.

Chicken satay sticks

4 chicken breast fillets, cubed

MARINADE

2–3 garlic cloves, peeled, crushed and finely chopped

1 level tbsp soft brown sugar

1 tsp ground coriander

$1/2$ tsp ground cumin

2 tbsp light soy sauce

juice of 1 lime

2 tbsp coconut milk (see Tip)

SAUCE

4 tbsp good-quality crunchy peanut butter

4 tbsp coconut cream (see Tip)

a dash of chilli sauce

1 level tbsp sweet mango chutney

NUTRITION NOTES

High in protein and B vitamins. Coconut milk and cream are high in saturated fat but it is now thought that this particular type of saturate is fine!

SERVING SUGGESTION

Serve with green salad and rice or noodles.

Serves 4 children

Suitable for ages 5 years +

✳ **Will freeze before cooking**

Nutrition   ⬭ Fat   ⬭ Saturates   ⬭ Sugar   ⬭ Salt

1 Blend all the marinade ingredients together and marinate the chicken pieces in a shallow non-metallic bowl for several hours, covered.

2 When ready to cook, thread the chicken on to satay sticks and grill for about 10 minutes, turning from time to time and basting with the leftover marinade.

3 Meanwhile combine all the sauce ingredients in a bowl (this is easier if the peanut butter is warm). Serve the sticks with the sauce.

Variations

You can use pork or beef instead of chicken. If you are in a hurry you can buy ready-made satay sauce.

TIP

Buy a can of coconut milk (widely available), and keep it upright. When you open the can, spoon off the thick coconut cream which will be on the top, reserve and use in the sauce. You will find the thin coconut milk underneath, so use this in the marinade. Leftovers can be used in a Thai curry for the grown-ups.

Kebab and BBQ ideas

- Netmums member Sarah sent in this idea for barbecuing mushrooms. 'Halve some mushrooms, peel and chop some garlic, put on foil, drizzle over some red wine and olive oil, make a parcel of the foil and barbecue until tender. Mmmm!'

- You can also BBQ whole large flat mushrooms if you prefer. Mix chopped garlic and parsley with butter and fill the cavity before putting in the foil – like garlic bread without the bread!

- Whole corn on the cobs are gorgeous wrapped in foil and cooked on a medium BBQ. They take about 20 minutes.

- Judith says, 'Fruit kebabs taste wonderful and make the ideal outdoor dessert. Just chop suitable fruits (e.g. peaches, apple, banana, orange) into bite-sized chunks, marinade in lemon juice for a while then thread on to sticks, brush with runny honey and heat up on the BBQ for a short while only. Rich in vitamin C and carotene!'

Netmums members Lisa, Julie and Mia all think the Cypriot cheese halloumi is a must for any barbecue. 'Chop it into chunks and include it in your vegetable kebabs. It doesn't melt like most cheeses,' they say.

Standalone Salads

'My children have started eating *lettuces and other salad ingredients* since we grew just a few vegetables in a corner of our garden. Their *delight* in growing and *waiting to eat* a "real live lettuce" had them arguing over who would get the biggest leaf. It was *a real turning point* and now they are very proud to tell their friends that *they love salad.*' Donna, mum to Sam and Emma

These salads can be served as part of an outdoor buffet if you feel like a change from lighting the barbecue.

Potato and ham salad

Serves 4 children

Suitable for ages 1 year +

Nutrition ◗ Fat ◗ Saturates ◗ Sugar ◗ Salt

400g cooked potato (see Tips, below)

150g lean ham, diced

3 tbsp mayonnaise

2 tbsp natural low-fat bio yoghurt

a squeeze of lemon juice

salt and pepper

1–2 tbsp chopped herbs (e.g. parsley, chives)

TIPS
The yoghurt gives a lighter dressing and reduces the total saturated fat content.

Salad potatoes such as Charlotte are good for this but you can use virtually any other sort of potato if you like. If cooking the potatoes fresh for this salad, let them cool right down before tossing with the dressing.

1 Dice the potato into a serving bowl and stir in the ham.

2 Mix together the mayo, yoghurt, lemon juice, a pinch of salt and some black pepper, and the herbs. Combine with the potato and ham, and chill before serving.

Variations
Use lean cooked bacon or cooked chicken breast pieces instead of the ham. Or, for serving with barbecued meats, omit the meat element altogether. Small pieces of other vegetables can be added – e.g. sweetcorn kernels or cold broad beans.

Another potato salad from Netmums member Jenny from Bromley: 'Combine *new potatoes*, crushed *garlic* and some *olive oil* in a baking dish. Bake in a hot oven for 30 minutes or until the potatoes are brown and crisp. Meanwhile cook *a few rashers of bacon* in a frying pan until crisp. Toss the potatoes, bacon and cooked chopped chicken in a bowl with a *couple of tbsp of mayonnaise, chives* and a *tbsp of seed mustard* (optional).'

Roast vegetable and chicken salad

Serves 4 children

Suitable for ages 1 year +

Nutrition ⬤ Fat ◯ Saturates ◯ Sugar ⬤ Salt

800g assorted Mediterranean vegetables (e.g. red pepper, courgette, red onion, aubergine, tomato)

2 nice fresh garlic cloves, left whole

2–3 tbsp olive oil

3 skinless chicken breast fillets, each cut into 4 pieces

salt and pepper

1 tbsp balsamic vinegar

2 tbsp fresh Mediterranean herbs (e.g. basil, oregano)

NUTRITION NOTES
Excellent amounts of vitamin C, beta-carotene, fibre and all kinds of goodies in here.

SERVING SUGGESTION
This goes very well with garlic or crusty bread.

1   Preheat the oven to 180ºC/350ºF/Gas 4.

2   Prepare, cut and chop the vegetables as necessary, into large bite-sized pieces and put them, with the garlic, in a roasting dish. Toss very well with 2 tbsp of the olive oil so that they form one layer without too much spare space.

3   Roast in the preheated oven for 15 minutes, then add the chicken pieces and toss everything thoroughly again. Roast for a further 25 minutes or until the chicken and vegetables are cooked through and golden.

4   Allow to cool slightly then tip into a serving dish and toss with the balsamic vinegar, remaining olive oil and herbs to serve.

Variations
Omit the chicken and use the vegetable salad alone with barbecued lamb chops or steaks.

TIP
The roast garlic flesh can be squeezed from the whole cloves and stirred into the vinegar and oil before adding to the salad, for those who like it.

Tuna and egg salad

Serves 4 children

Suitable for ages 1 year +

Nutrition   ● Fat   ◑ Saturates   ○ Sugar   ○ Salt

*300g fresh tuna steak or good-
quality tuna canned in spring
water (see Nutrition notes)*

4 medium free-range eggs

75g green beans, topped and tailed

200g cooked salad potatoes, diced

2 medium tomatoes, chopped

4 spring onions, chopped

*4 tbsp olive oil French dressing
(see page 100)*

NUTRITION NOTES

If using canned tuna, avoid those
canned in brine as they are very salty. If
you can't find spring water cans, use
tuna in oil and drain it very well. Fresh
tuna is a good source of omega-3 oils.

1   Cook the tuna by searing in a non-stick pan or under the
grill for about 2 $\frac{1}{2}$ minutes a side then flake. Or, if using,
drain the canned tuna and pat the chunks dry.

2   Meanwhile, hard-boil the eggs for about 7 minutes and
cook the green beans in the same water for 4 minutes.
Drain the eggs and beans. Cool the eggs, shell them and
cut into quarters.

3   When everything is ready, arrange the fish, egg quarters,
beans, potato, tomatoes and onions on a serving platter
and sprinkle over the dressing.

Variations

Most children don't enjoy olives but if yours do, add 8–12
stoned halved olives to the dish. You can also sprinkle fresh
parsley over if you like. If you haven't any beans you can
omit them and add some crisp Little Gem hearts, cut into
thin wedges, instead.

French dressing

6 parts olive oil

1 part red or white wine vinegar

1 part balsamic vinegar

1 tsp caster sugar

1 tsp Dijon mustard

freshly ground black pepper

1/2 level tsp salt

1 Combine all the ingredients in a screw-top jar.

2 Shake well before using. Will store in the fridge for several weeks.

Tips for outdoor salads

- Don't leave salads containing meat or fish hanging around too long in hot sun – they could build up bacteria which may cause food poisoning.

- Leaf salads wilt easily in the sun – choose the more robust leaves such as Little Gem hearts.

- Sometimes children enjoy very simple finger salads out of doors – a plate of crudités to eat with a burger may be just the job.

- Once the initial serving is done, put lids over all salads to keep off flies and to make sure the salads don't dry out before second helpings.

Side Dishes

All these side salads go well with any barbecued meats or fish.

Crunchy pasta

Serves 4–6 children

Suitable for ages 5 years + (leave out the nuts and seeds and it's suitable for 1 year +)

Nutrition   ⬤ Fat   ⬤ Saturates   ⬤ Sugar   ⬤ Salt

250g tricolour pasta shapes of
  choice

1 medium red pepper

1 x 7cm piece cucumber

2–4 spring onions, depending on
  size, trimmed and chopped

60g sweetcorn kernels, lightly
  cooked

8 cherry tomatoes, quartered

25g pine nuts

25g sunflower seeds

2 tbsp mayonnaise

3 tbsp natural low-fat bio yoghurt

salt and pepper

NUTRITION NOTES
This pasta is full of goodness and looks
pretty. If you use semi-wholewheat or
wholewheat pasta you will increase the
fibre and vitamin B content.

1   Cook the pasta according to packet instructions and when
    just cooked, drain and allow to cool until just warm.
    Meanwhile, seed and chop the pepper into small pieces;
    quarter the cucumber lengthways, seed and chop.

2   When the pasta is ready, tip into a serving bowl and add the
    vegetables, nuts and seeds and stir well.

3   Beat together the mayo and yoghurt, add a little seasoning
    if liked, and stir into the pasta. Chill to serve.

Variations

You can add chopped celery for even more crunch. If you
have time, toast the pine kernels to add flavour and crunch.
Simply heat a non-stick frying pan over a high heat and stir-
fry the kernels until they begin to brown. Remove
immediately from the pan (otherwise they will burn).

Fruity couscous

Serves 4–6 children

Suitable for ages 5 years + (leave out the almonds and it's suitable for 1 year +)

Nutrition   ⬤ Fat   ⬤ Saturates   ⬤ Sugar   ⬤ Salt

approx. 500ml low-salt vegetable stock (see Tip)

225g couscous

50g sultanas or raisins

50g ready-to-eat dried apricots

50g small red seedless grapes

50g flaked almonds, toasted

2–3 tbsp finely chopped parsley

NUTRITION NOTES
Couscous isn't very high in nutrients or fibre but it is a good, harmless carbohydrate which most children enjoy, and its blandness is a good foil for tasty and acidic additions. The dried fruits add iron and fibre while the almonds are high in essential fats.

TIP
You can get low-salt vegetable bouillon from most health-food stores.

1   Boil the stock and pour it over the couscous in a heatproof bowl. Allow to stand for 10 minutes or until all the stock is absorbed and the couscous is tender. You may need slightly more stock (or water) if the mix looks too dry. Fluff up gently with a fork.

2   Now stir all the fruit and almonds and the parsley into the couscous.

Variations

You can use saffron water (1 sachet saffron threads, soaked in a little water for 15 minutes then added to the boiling water). For a higher-calorie salad, add 1–2 tbsp light salad oil when you add the fruit.

Another great couscous salad addition is chopped, sautéed sweet peppers and red onion.

Mexican rice

Netmums member Tam says: *'This is delicious on its own, as part of a buffet, or served with sausages. It can be served warm or cold.'*

Serves 4–8 children/adults

Suitable for ages 1 year +

Nutrition   Fat   Saturates   Sugar   Salt

1 medium onion, peeled and finely chopped

1 green or yellow pepper, seeded and diced into 5mm pieces

1–2 tbsp olive oil or groundnut oil

250g tasty mushrooms (more if you like!), diced

about 275g long-grain rice

1 x 400g can chopped tomatoes

a dash of mushroom ketchup

1 beef, chicken or vegetable stock cube, made up with 500ml boiling water

NUTRITION NOTES

The basic salad is a healthy dish. Make it even more nutritious by using brown rice (which will need longer cooking, see Rice, page 63). Stock cubes are high in salt; fresh, chilled stock is a lower-salt alternative.

1   Sauté the onion and pepper in half the oil in a large pan over a medium-high heat for a few minutes until the onion looks transparent.

2   Add the mushrooms and the rest of the oil and stir for a few more minutes. When all the vegetables are soft, add the rice and cook dry for about a minute, stirring.

3   Add the chopped tomatoes and ketchup, and stir well then add the stock. Let this cook/simmer, covered, for about half an hour or until the rice is soft and has absorbed the liquid.

Variations

You can add almost what you like to this rice salad: small cooked peas, pieces of cooked chicken or ham. If serving cold you can drizzle over a little French dressing or olive oil and stir in if you like.

Potato wedges

Serves 4 children

Suitable for ages 1 year +

Nutrition ⬤ Fat ◯ Saturates ◯ Sugar ⬤ Salt

---

*2 x 275g (medium to large) baking
potatoes or 550g potatoes,
washed*

2 tbsp olive oil

salt and pepper

NUTRITION NOTES

These potato wedges are a great
alternative to fried chips or oven chips.
They contain no trans fats and will be
lower in total fat than any commercial
potato fry/bake varieties. Baked chips
are a good source of vitamin C.

SERVING SUGGESTION

Ideal with any grilled foods, can be used
as a scoop for dips and great with all
kinds of fried or baked fish and chicken.

1   Preheat the oven to 190°C/375°F/Gas 5.

2   Cut the potatoes lengthwise into wedges. Each potato
should make about 12 wedges. Don't worry about the skin,
just leave it on. Dry them with kitchen paper or a tea-towel
and put in a large bowl. Dribble the olive oil over and
combine thoroughly with your hands.

3   Now arrange in a single layer on a baking tray and cook for
about 40 minutes until crisp and golden.

Variations

To cut down on the baking time, parboil the wedges of
potato for 5–6 minutes first. Dry with a tea-towel or kitchen
paper before coating with oil as above. Cook the chips for
about 25 minutes.

Older children may enjoy the wedges coated (before
baking) with various types of seasoning – e.g. Cajun
seasoning, BBQ seasoning or garlic seasoning. Be aware
that most dried seasonings that come in jars are quite high
in salt.

Hot wraps

'I love wraps and serve them all the time, especially if fussy children are coming to tea. They can just fill their wraps with the bits they like and leave out the bits they don't like. Though they do often find it so much fun that they forget that they don't like vegetables. I like to watch their parents' jaws drop at what their kids have just eaten!' Sara from Oxfordshire

Thank goodness for wraps! When kids get fed up with sliced bread and rolls they are a blessing – children always find them so much fun to eat, especially outdoors. Once you've decided on a filling, just plonk it in the middle of the flatbread, turn up one side, then roll and there you have it – a wrap! Cover with some kitchen paper, a paper napkin or foil and it's not very messy to eat. If you haven't any flatbreads for the wraps, use pittas: carefully split them along one short end and fill. Wraps can have cold fillings (see page 107) but they are even better hot. And some hot fillings are still good when they have gone cold – so what could be more forgiving for an outdoor supper or barbie! Try mixing small pieces of any grilled or barbecued meat or poultry, with a little sauce (e.g. mayo, salsa, ketchup, yoghurt) and some favourite salad items (e.g. tomato slices, cucumber, iceberg lettuce).

Lamb and pine nut wraps

1 tbsp light olive oil

400g fillet of lamb, cut into thin strips

1 large beef tomato, skinned, seeded and chopped

1 large garlic clove, peeled and well crushed

30g pine nuts, toasted (see page 101)

200g Greek yoghurt

4 large wraps or pittas

NUTRITION NOTES

Based on a Turkish recipe, this is great as a pitta filling and very moreish. It is rich in vitamins B, C and E and contains plenty of iron.

Serves 4 children

Suitable for ages 5 years + (leave out the nuts and it's suitable for 1 year +)

Nutrition   ◖ Fat   ◖ Saturates   ◖ Sugar   ◖ Salt

1   Heat the oil in a heavy non-stick frying pan, and sauté the lamb strips in two batches over a high heat for a few minutes until browned on the outside. Remove with a slotted spoon to a bowl.

2   Stir-fry the tomato and garlic together in the same pan for a couple of minutes then add to the meat in the bowl, along with the toasted pine nuts. Stir in the yoghurt.

3   Make up the wraps or pittas, and serve straightaway.

Variations
You can use chicken instead of lamb.

Mexican chicken wraps

Serves 4 children

Suitable for ages 1 year +

Nutrition ⬭ Fat ⬭ Saturates ⬭ Sugar ⬭ Salt

*2–3 chicken breast fillets, sliced
quite thinly*

1 dsp fajita seasoning

*1 1/2 tbsp groundnut or other light
oil*

*1 red pepper and 1 yellow pepper,
seeded and thinly sliced*

*4 tbsp ready-made mild red pepper
sauce or tomato sauce*

4 large tortilla wraps or pittas

2–3 tbsp thick natural yoghurt

NUTRITION NOTES
Lovely healthy finger food, rich in
protein, vitamin C, carotenes and fibre.

1 Sprinkle the chicken pieces with half the fajita seasoning
and cook them in half the oil in a non-stick frying pan until
cooked through and golden. Remove with a slotted spoon to
a plate.

2 Add the peppers to the pan with the rest of the oil and
seasoning, and stir-fry over a medium-high heat for 8–10
minutes or until they are tender and turning brown. Return
the chicken to the pan, add the red pepper sauce and cook
for a minute or two, stirring.

3 Fill the wraps (or pittas) with the mixture and drizzle over
the yoghurt.

Variations

You can use other coloured peppers. You can add chopped
fresh chilli to the pan with the peppers. You can use soured
cream instead of the yoghurt. You can use pork or beef
instead of the chicken, or use no meat and add some nuts,
for veggies over five years.

More Netmums wrap ideas

Netmums member Sofie from Calderdale has a very simple healthy wrap filling recipe. She says: 'Fry some chicken breast pieces in a tiny bit of olive oil in a non-stick pan. Meanwhile grate some carrot and some cheese and steam some fresh broccoli spears. Let your kids fill the wraps themselves.

'You can use just about any veg in it, raw or lightly cooked, and any sort of meat (or refried beans for vegetarians). I find that the more variety I offer, the more veg the kids will actually eat: put out some grated carrot, spinach, mangetouts, broccoli, tomatoes, nuts and beansprouts , and each kid might only select half the foods, but it still adds up to a lot of vegetables they are eating. They just can't resist including lots of different items because it is so fun to sprinkle it on and wrap it up. I serve it with salsa and soured cream.'

Netmums member Crissy from Kingston says: 'Making chicken wraps is even easier if you make a foil bag and pop chicken breasts in with either a splash of water or my fave balsamic vinegar and pop in the oven, then there's no fat at all. I fill small dishes with loads of different veg and cheese. The kids love it and the mums can't believe what I get their darlings to eat.

'Hold some chicken pieces back and stir-fry them with some paprika for the grown-up version. They are so quick to cook you can still all eat together.

'Throw all leftovers into a big bowl and use as salad for yourself the next day.'

Winter warmers

A comfortable, warm, safe haven is what we want 'home' to represent for our children, and on cold winter days a large part of that comes from providing satisfying hot dinners. Soups, stews, casseroles, bakes and most pies really are easy-cook dishes. Some take a bit longer than others, but none needs a lot of fussing over. This chapter aims to provide the encouragement and inspiration for the traditional and classic meals of the colder months, and to show that they really aren't difficult. The long lists of variations prove that these recipes can easily be adapted to suit your own family.

Soups

'I'm not a hugely enthusiastic cook – I do it out of necessity mainly – but when I serve up bowls of steaming home-made soup full of goodness and wholesomeness with fresh crusty bread for dipping, I feel – just for a moment – like a truly great mum.' Emma, mum to Sophie, Hugh and Jack

Many people are frightened of making their own soup, thinking somehow that it must be difficult to pull off – but the truth is that it couldn't be easier! Well, perhaps there are a few that need a higher level of skill and care, but mostly you just chop things up, stick them in a pan with some stock, cook, blend, and there you have it: something deliciously warm and comforting, inexpensive, lovely to look at – and a nutritious meal that will have the children asking for it time and again. Even vegetable haters. What more can you ask? Like stir-fries, most soup-making involves following a simple blueprint that goes like this:

1　Chop up onion and sauté until transparent.

2　Add your other vegetables (and meat or fish if using), all prepared and chopped. Stir for a bit.

3　Add your herbs, seasonings and stock, stir and bring to a simmer.

4　Put a lid on and simmer until everything is tender – usually no more than half an hour, sometimes much less.

5　Allow to cool in the pan a bit and then, if you have an electric blender, blend either all of the soup for a smooth, thick result suitable for children of all ages, or just half of it for a thick soup that still has some texture. Or, if you have no blender or prefer mega-chunky soup, just leave it as it is and serve or just mash some of the chunks a bit with a large fork.

6　Reheat if necessary and serve with bread and garnishes of your choice.

Honestly, it's so easy.

The soup recipes that follow are five easy ones to start with, all great for the colder months, but some are good in summer too. Our suggestions for variations will prevent boredom ever setting in – but do try your own combinations; don't be afraid!

Soup tips

- Aim to use about half 'solid' items such as vegetables/pulses and half stock, but this isn't an exact science so don't worry too much if you have different proportions.

- Once you've blended the soup you can always add extra liquid (hot water or stock) if it seems too thick. But you can't easily thicken it up – so if you aren't sure about how much liquid to use if you're making a soup without a recipe, add a little less than you think.

- Some flavours marry particularly well together – e.g. carrot and tomato; potato and leek; potato and broccoli; peppers and tomato – but mixed vegetable soups are very adaptable.

- Extra items, such as ground nuts, grated or crumbled cheese, can be added at the end of cooking time: they just need to melt into the soup rather than be cooked.

- Many soups contain onion and tomatoes: the onions add depth and sweetness while the tomatoes add both sweetness, colour and acidity.

- Leftover cooked vegetables can quickly be made into a soup using leftover gravy, extra stock and a can of chopped tomatoes. Heat together then blend.

- Most soups will freeze well – use strong ziplock bags or safely lidded containers.

- Don't add more than a pinch of salt, especially if serving to younger children. Herbs, spices, garlic and other flavourings should mean it isn't necessary.

- For main-meal soups, include a source of protein – e.g. beans, lentils, chicken or cheese.

- If you don't have a blender, the addition of floury potatoes to your soup mix helps to thicken it up. Or you could use a little instant dried mashed potato or canned butter beans for the same effect.

Stock for soups

Top chefs make their own stock, and you can too if you have the time. A quick veg stock can be made by roughly chopping celery, carrot, and leek into a pan with water, pepper and some parsley and simmering for 30 minutes; strain through a sieve. Otherwise you can use fresh chilled stock from the supermarket, which is often quite good but expensive. Then of course, most of us use stock cubes. These can make perfectly decent stock but, a word of warning, lots of them are very high in salt which isn't great for children. So either use double the quantity of liquid stated per cube or seek out low-salt stock bouillon. The nutrition panels on the following recipes rate salt content on the basis of low-salt stock. If you want to add salt to any of the recipes, do, but make sure to taste first and only add a very little. Make sure to match your stock to your ingredients (i.e. don't use a beef stock cube for vegetable soup or a fish stock cube for chicken soup!)

Butternut squash soup

A very easy soup from Ashwini, who says: *'Butternut squash is deliciously sweet and has a soft texture – two reasons why it is really popular with children.'*

You can use butternut squash or any other firm squash or orange-fleshed pumpkin for this recipe.

Serves 4–6 children

Suitable for ages 6 months + (1 year + if not low-salt stock)

❄ **Will freeze**

Nutrition   ⬭ Fat   ⬭ Saturates   ⬭ Sugar   ⬭ Salt

1 medium onion, peeled and finely chopped

1–2 tbsp light olive oil or groundnut oil

1 garlic clove, peeled and finely chopped

1 medium butternut squash, peeled, seeded as necessary (easy using a large fairly flat-bowled spoon), and cut into cubes

1 tsp ground turmeric (optional)

800ml vegetable stock

NUTRITION NOTES

Squash and carrot are rich in beta-carotene for healthy heart and good eyesight.

1   Sauté the onion in the oil in a non-stick frying pan for about 8 minutes over medium heat, stirring occasionally, until transparent. Add the garlic and stir for a minute or two.

2   Add the butternut squash cubes to the frying pan with the turmeric (if using) and sauté for a further 5 minutes.

3   Add the stock and simmer for 25–30 minutes or until the squash is tender.

4   Allow to cool a little then purée in a blender. Reheat to serve and garnish with a little grated cheese if liked.

Variations

Netmums' member Nic from Stockport has a similar recipe but using 500g chopped carrots instead of the squash. Omit the turmeric and add ground coriander seeds instead. Nic garnishes this with swirls of cream or yoghurt.

Another version of this last variation will give you carrot and orange soup. Replace 400ml of the stock with 250ml chopped canned tomatoes and the juice of 1 large orange. Add ½ tsp each of coriander seeds and cumin seeds.

Lastly, you can use peeled cubed sweet potato (the orange-fleshed type) instead of either the squash or the carrot.

Spicy lentil soup

Sent in by 'Sean's grandma'.

Serves 4 children

Suitable for ages 6 months + (1 year + if not low-salt stock)

❄ **Will freeze**

Nutrition ◓ Fat   ◯ Saturates   ◯ Sugar   ◯ Salt

2 tbsp olive oil

1 onion, peeled and chopped

2 garlic cloves, peeled and
  crushed

1 red pepper, seeded and chopped

$^1/_2$ tsp ground cumin

$^1/_2$ tsp ground ginger

$^1/_2$ tsp ground coriander

1 x 400g can chopped tomatoes

75g dry split red lentils

550ml vegetable stock

freshly ground black pepper

NUTRITION NOTES
Full of vitamin C, carotene, and fibre.
Red lentils are a good source of protein.

1 Heat the oil in a large non-stick frying pan. Add the onion
   and garlic and cook until softened but not browned, about
   10 minutes.

2 Add the pepper and spices and stir-fry for about 2 minutes.

3 Add the remaining ingredients and bring to the boil. Cover,
   reduce the heat and simmer for about 25–30 minutes.

4 Allow to cool slightly, then blend in an electric blender.
   Reheat to serve. Garnish with fresh coriander leaves or a
   pinch of paprika if liked.

Variations
You can use a 400g can of ready-cooked red lentils (well rinsed
and drained) if you like and reduce the cooking time by 10
minutes. You can use a jar of passata (sieved tomatoes)
instead of the chopped tomatoes.

Wholesome tomato soup

Sent in by Emma from Sutton, who says: *'This is an excellent recipe for getting some vegetables into your toddler's diet. It's a winner with my fussy two-year-old. Serve it with some wholemeal toast for a good all-round meal.'*

There are dozens of different recipes for tomato soup (see Variations) but this one is particularly tasty and has a bit more filling ability than many because of the addition of potato.

Serves 4 children

Suitable for ages 6 months +

✳ **Will freeze**

Nutrition   ⬭ Fat   ⬭ Saturates   ⬭ Sugar   ⬭ Salt

1 onion, peeled and chopped

2 tbsp olive oil

2 garlic cloves, peeled and crushed

1 large carrot, peeled and sliced

1 large potato, peeled and sliced

1 red pepper, seeded and chopped

1 x 400g can chopped tomatoes

700ml vegetable stock

1 tsp caster sugar

NUTRITION NOTES
Onions and garlic are great food for kids in winter as they contain various compounds which are antibacterial and antioxidant.

1 Fry the onion in the olive oil for a couple of minutes until transparent. Then add the garlic, carrot, potato and red pepper and cook for a further 5 minutes.

2 Add the remaining ingredients, bring up to boiling point and then simmer for 20 minutes or until the vegetables are soft.

3 Allow to cool a little, blend in an electric blender and reheat gently to serve. Garnish with chives or parsley if liked, or a swirl of cream.

Variations

For a lighter soup (e.g. as part of a bonfire night spread) omit the potato.

You can also leave out the pepper if you don't happen to have one around. Or, if you don't have any carrots, you can omit them and use two red peppers instead of one.

Lastly, you can use a can of baked beans in tomato sauce instead of the potato for richness, thickness and a source of protein.

Chicken soup

Serves 4 children

Suitable for ages 1 year +

❄ **Will freeze**

Nutrition ⬤ Fat   ⬤ Saturates   ◯ Sugar   ◯ Salt

*2 free-range or organic chicken leg
portions (on the bone)*

100g swede, peeled and chopped

*2 large carrots, peeled and
chopped*

*1 medium potato, peeled and
chopped*

1 large leek, chopped

2 celery stalks, chopped

800ml vegetable or chicken stock

freshly ground black pepper

1 tbsp chopped parsley

NUTRITION NOTES

Chicken soup has long been regarded
as a cure-all – and now scientific study
has found that it really does boost the
immune system and speed recovery
after illness.

1 Put the chicken portions in a large pan with all the
ingredients except the parsley. Bring to a simmer, put the
lid on and cook for an hour on a low heat.

2 Take the chicken pieces from the pan and allow to cool until
you can handle them. Remove the skin and shred the
chicken into pieces. Return the flesh to the soup pan and
throw the rest away.

3 Bring back to the simmer and cook for 5 minutes. Now the
soup is ready to serve (don't blend), garnished with the
parsley.

Variations

Use parsnip or sweet potato instead of swede, or just use
one extra carrot.

Use one medium onion instead of the leek. You can use
breast portions on the bone if you like but the meat will be a
little more dry.

Chunky vegetable soup

Serves 4 children

Suitable for ages 1 year +

❋ **Will freeze** (but reduce total cooking time and finish when thawed)

Nutrition ⬭ Fat ⬭ Saturates ⬭ Sugar ⬭ Salt

1 tbsp olive oil

1 medium onion, peeled and finely chopped

2 medium carrots, peeled and roughly chopped

100g white cabbage, chopped

125g broccoli, cut into small florets

1 medium courgette, topped, tailed and sliced then halved

1 x 400g can green or brown lentils, well rinsed and drained

1 x 400g can chopped tomatoes

350ml vegetable stock

NUTRITION NOTES

There are a wide variety of plant chemicals in here as well as plenty of fibre, vitamins and minerals. The beans provide protein and carbohydrate so it really is a complete meal.

TIP

Some dried pulses other than lentils (e.g. kidney beans) need about 10 minutes of fast boiling to remove toxins. Follow the packet instructions for cooking – our advice is to pre-cook all dried pulses apart from lentils before adding to the soup.

1 Heat the oil in a large non-stick lidded pan and sauté the onion for 10 minutes or until transparent. Add the carrot, cabbage, broccoli and courgette, and stir for a minute or two.

2 Add the lentils, tomatoes and stock, stir well, bring to a simmer, put the lid on and cook for 25–30 minutes or until everything is tender.

3 Remove half of the soup to an electric blender and blend for a few seconds then return the blended soup to the pan, stir well and reheat. Serve, garnished if liked with some grated cheese on top.

Variations

• You can use a variety of other pulses in this soup – older children will like red kidney beans for instance. Try black-eye beans or cannellini beans too, or a can of mixed beans. If you want to use dried lentils, add around 125g dried weight, increase the stock to 500ml and cook for an extra 10 minutes or until the pulses are tender.

• The veggies in this really are a moveable feast – you can mix and match as you like. Green beans, leeks, peppers will all go in this. Serve with crusty bread for a great main course.

Netmums member Jacqui suggests a quick roast vegetable soup, using odds and ends of veggies in your fridge. 'Chop them, then put in a roasting pan and coat in olive oil. Roast at 180°C/350°F/Gas 4 for half an hour and then tip into your soup pan.' You can now follow the recipe above at step 2.

Hallowe'en and Bonfire Night

'I remember this time of year from my childhood as being a magical and exciting time. I'd like my children to also remember baked potatoes and fried chicken eaten with friends, outside in the dark either dressed up or watching the fireworks.' Helen, mum to Thomas and Samuel

Bonfire baked potatoes

Potatoes cooked either fully or partially at the base of the bonfire always taste so much more delicious than those cooked in the oven or microwave. Have one medium baking potato for everyone. Wash the potatoes, dry them thoroughly and make a split down one side. Wrap each potato in foil so that the foil 'join' runs along the cut side of the potato. Cook in a preheated hot oven (220°C/425°F/Gas 7) for half an hour and then, wearing oven gloves of course, transfer them to the hot embers at the base of the bonfire for an hour or until cooked through (test one yourself with a sharp knife or skewer to see). When cooked, open the foil and squeeze the potato until it opens then add your choice of toppings/fillings or let the children choose.

Variations

- If you have plenty of patience and the bonfire coals are kind, you can do the whole process in the bonfire – but experience shows that often the potatoes either refuse to cook through to the centre (because the fire embers aren't hot enough) or they burn (too hot! – wrapping them in the foil, however, helps prevent burning). Medium spuds will probably cook this way in around $1\frac{1}{2}$–2 hours.

- Instead of part-baking in the traditional oven, you could microwave the potatoes for 7–8 minutes on high before wrapping them in the foil.

- For older children and grown-ups the potatoes crisp up brilliantly and taste even better if, after washing them, and while they are still damp, you dip them lightly in flaked sea salt. Small children shouldn't be eating this much salt.

Continued

Fillings/toppings ideal for eating round the bonfire

- Butter
- Garlic butter (peel and well crush some good fresh garlic cloves and combine with slightly warmed butter in a bowl – ratio 100g butter to 3–4 garlic cloves)
- Herb butter (chop some soft fresh herbs – e.g. parsley, tarragon – and combine with warmed butter)
- Grated cheese
- Ketchup

Fillings/toppings more suitable for eating on a plate

- Drained tuna mixed with mayo and cooked/canned sweetcorn kernels
- Coleslaw (make your own by mixing together finely shredded white cabbage, grated carrot, grated onion, sultanas in proportion 4:2:1:1, and adding enough mayo/yoghurt to moisten thoroughly)
- Scrambled egg (make sure it is thoroughly cooked for young children: see page 81)
- Chilli con carne (see page 152)
- Baked beans
- Prawns in prawn cocktail sauce (make your own by mixing together natural yoghurt, mayonnaise and tomato ketchup with a dash of lemon juice if liked)
- Crispy chopped bacon and sautéed chopped mushroom

Home-made coleslaw with cheese

Show a child cabbage and he or she will go 'yuck' – but show that child a creamy coleslaw and it is often a different story altogether!

Serves 4 children

Suitable for ages 1 year +

Nutrition   ⬭ Fat   ⬭ Saturates   ⬭ Sugar   ⬭ Salt

300g firm fresh white cabbage, or mix of white and red

2 medium carrots

1 shallot or small onion

75g sultanas or ready-to-eat dried apricots

4 tbsp low-fat natural bio yoghurt

2 tbsp light mayonnaise

juice of ¼ lemon

freshly ground black pepper

75g Cheddar, freshly grated

NUTRITION NOTES
Plenty of vitamin C, fibre and potassium in this salad as well as calcium.

TIP
Make sure you use a nice big mixing bowl so the cabbage doesn't fall over the edges. Chill to serve.

1   Using a sharp knife finely slice the cabbage across the grain and then chop into 2cm lengths; tip into a large mixing bowl. Peel and grate the carrots on a medium grater and add to the bowl. Peel and grate the onion on a fine grater (or very finely chop it) and add to the bowl.

2   Tip the fruit into the bowl and stir thoroughly to combine.

3   In another bowl, combine the yoghurt, mayo, lemon juice and pepper and then add the cheese to this mix and stir well.

4   Now spoon all the cheesey dressing into the cabbage mix and stir very thoroughly.

Traditional American fried chicken

Sent in by Kelly from Cambridge.

Serves 4–8 children

Suitable for ages 1 year +

❄ **Will freeze**

Nutrition   ⬤ Fat   ◔ Saturates   ◯ Sugar   ◯ Salt

4 skinless chicken breast fillets,
  sliced into strips or nuggets

light olive oil

BATTER

75g plain flour

$1/2$ tsp baking powder

$1/2$ tsp salt

$1/2$ tsp paprika (just leave it out if
  you haven't got any)

75ml beer

1 medium egg

1 garlic clove, peeled and minced
  or very finely chopped

NUTRITION NOTES
Chicken is a great source of protein and
B vitamins. Olive oil is a good oil to use
for hot frying as it doesn't oxidise.

SERVING SUGGESTION
Other than Bonfire Night, this is nice
served with salad, new potatoes and
coleslaw.

1   For the batter, mix the dry ingredients together and the wet ingredients – including the garlic – together. Add wet to dry and mix with a fork until blended (if you get any lumps use a whisk until they disappear).

2   Heat a large, deep frying pan containing about 1cm depth of light olive oil (or other vegetable oil) until smoke is coming from the oil (i.e. until it's HOT).

3   Dip the chicken pieces in the batter (several at a time), coat thoroughly and use tongs to put into the hot oil. Add another lot and then turn the first pieces when golden brown – they take about 2–3 minutes each side. Transfer to a plate lined with kitchen paper.

Cowboy chicken

Sent in by Laura from Liverpool, who says: 'This is such a quick easy dish and children love picking up chicken legs in their hands and not having to bother with knives and forks.

'Put as many chicken drumsticks, thighs or wings in an ovenproof dish as you need. Squeeze a couple of lemons over them and squash several cloves of garlic (one per person is a good guide but it depends on your taste). Marinate in the fridge for a couple of hours. When you're ready, pop them in the oven preheated to 180°C/350°F/Gas 4 and cook for around 40 minutes, or until the chicken is cooked through.'

SERVING SUGGESTION

For occasions other than round the bonfire, you can serve with chips, rice or baked beans and your favourite vegetables.

Variation

You can vary the marinade to introduce different flavours: maybe add honey to give them a sweet glaze, or be adventurous and try the juice of an orange and a bit of ground ginger.

One-pot curried sausage and beans

Sent in by Donna from Leeds, who says: 'This recipe is really easy and it is really yummy. Even my 13-month-old baby loves it. I add a few chopped veggies when doing it for the little one. I am a vegetarian and so I often make it with veggie sausages, but either meat or veg is good. Enjoy!'

The recipe is fine for a bonfire night party as it can be served in heatproof plastic dishes and eaten with a spoon if necessary.

Serves 4 children

Suitable for ages 1 year +

❄ **Will freeze**

Nutrition ▭ Fat ▭ Saturates ▭ Sugar ▭ Salt

about 8 sausages

1 onion, peeled and chopped

a little olive oil or other vegetable oil

2 tsp curry powder (or to taste)

2 tsp turmeric

1 veg stock cube (low-salt if possible)

150ml boiling water

1 x 400g can baked beans (low-salt if possible)

TIP
Sausages vary so much in quality – it is worth paying a few pence extra to get those with a high lean meat content. Local butcher's sausages or organic sausages often taste excellent. If you are keeping an eye on your children's weight, you can buy extra-lean sausages.

1   Grill the sausages and chop each one into four pieces; keep warm.

2   Fry the onion in the oil on a low heat until soft.

3   Add the curry powder and turmeric to the onion pan, and cook for 1 minute, stirring.

4   Add the stock cube to the water and then add to the onion. Cook for 2 minutes then add the beans and sausages. Stir well and simmer for a few minutes until hot through.

Variations
You can add extra vegetables to this if you like – for example, mushrooms (add towards end of onion cooking time), cooked carrots (with the beans) or pieces of cooked broccoli (with the beans).

Cheesey corn triangles

Amanda from North Bucks sent this to the website: *'This recipe is great, a light cake-type bread to which you can add other ingredients: I've added peas and mushrooms in the past. It is an ideal snack and also great served with soup. My kiddies love it, I hope yours enjoy it too.'*

Serves 6 children

Suitable for ages 1 year +

Nutrition   ● Fat   ● Saturates   ○ Sugar   ◐ Salt

100g plain flour

100g semolina

1 tsp baking powder

2 medium eggs, beaten

100ml milk

50g butter

100g sweetcorn kernels, cooked

100g Cheddar cheese, grated

NUTRITION NOTES

For children who are reluctant to eat plain bread this makes a great savoury change. Ideal if you have a thin child and you want him or her to eat more carbs!

SERVING SUGGESTION

Try the triangles with any of our soup recipes (see pages 110–16).

TIP

Frozen or fresh sweetcorn kernels are best – canned kernels are usually quite salty.

1   Preheat the oven to 180°C/350°F/Gas 4 and lightly grease an 18–20cm round tin.

2   Mix the flour, semolina and baking powder together in a bowl, and beat the eggs and milk together in another bowl. Gently melt the butter in a saucepan over a low heat.

3   Add the sweetcorn and cheese to the dry flour mixture and then pour the eggy mixture into the bowl and add the butter. Mix the ingredients until well combined and then spoon the mixture into the baking tin.

4   Smooth the top and bake in the preheated oven for 20 minutes until golden brown and springy to the touch.

5   Leave to cool slightly then cut into wedges.

Other recipes for Hallowe'en and Bonfire Night

- Potato wedges served with a cheese dip (see pages 104 and 158)
- Chicken wraps (see page 164)
- Wedges of Spanish omelette (see pages 79–80)
- Chicken nuggets (see pages 48–9) served with a salsa dip or mayo
- Chicken satay sticks (see page 93)
- Pizza (see pages 74–7)
- Shepherd's pie (see pages 135–6: easy to eat with a spoon)

Pasta Bakes

Delicious and loved by almost all children, pasta bakes are easy and very variable. Warming and comforting, they are ideal as winter teatime meals.

Macaroni cheese

Serves 4 children

Suitable for ages 6 months +

❄ **Will freeze**

Nutrition ⬤ Fat   ⬤ Saturates   ⬜ Sugar   ⬜ Salt

300g macaroni

1 quantity cheese sauce (see page 134)

2 tbsp freshly grated Parmesan

3 tbsp stale breadcrumbs

NUTRITION NOTES

High in calcium, protein, B vitamins and potassium and plenty more. Yes, it is high in fat, but good nutrition for children is just as much about giving them what they do need, as it is about cutting back on fat, sugar and salt. The occasional home-cooked high saturated fat meal isn't a worry!

SERVING SUGGESTIONS

Serve with a crisp green salad, or peas, mangetouts or green beans.

1 Cook the macaroni in a large pan of boiling water with a pinch of salt and a dash of vegetable oil for 10 minutes or according to packet instructions. Drain and keep warm.

2 Meanwhile, preheat the oven to 190ºC/375ºF/Gas 5, and make the cheese sauce.

3 When the pasta and cheese sauce are ready, tip the pasta into a shallow baking dish and pour over the sauce. Stir well to combine.

4 Mix together the grated cheese and the crumbs and sprinkle evenly over the top. Bake in the preheated oven for 20–25 minutes or until the top is golden.

Variations

- Add some small pre-cooked broccoli florets to the macaroni before pouring over the sauce.

- Or thinly slice some tomato and arrange all round the edge of the dish on top of the sauce, before adding the grated cheese/crumb mix.

- For very hungry kids you can add some cooked sliced sausage or bacon to the mix, says Netmums member Sally from Warwick.

Tuna pasta bake

Serves 4 children

Suitable for ages 9 months +

☀ **Will freeze**

Nutrition ⬤ Fat ◑ Saturates ◯ Sugar ◑ Salt

250g pasta shapes of choice (see Tip)

salt and pepper

2 x 200g cans tuna in olive or sunflower oil

1 medium onion, peeled and finely chopped

1 large garlic clove, peeled and chopped

1 x 400g can chopped tomatoes

1 tsp mixed dried herbs

1 quantity cheese sauce (see page 134)

4 tbsp freshly grated mature Cheddar or Parmesan

NUTRITION NOTES

Tuna, both fresh and canned, is a good source of selenium, an antioxidant mineral that many children don't get enough of. Try not to use tuna canned in brine – it is too high in salt for children.

SERVING SUGGESTION

Just a salad, or you can add crusty bread for very hungry children.

TIP

Penne pasta or spirals work very well in this dish but you could also use farfalle (bows).

1 Cook the pasta in boiling water with a pinch of salt and a dash of vegetable oil according to packet instructions, usually about 10 minutes. Drain and keep warm.

2 Meanwhile, preheat the oven to 190°C/375°F/Gas 5.

3 Pour a little of the oil from the canned tuna into a pan and fry the onion over a medium heat for 8 minutes or so, until soft and transparent. Add the garlic and stir for a minute.

4 Add the tomatoes, herbs and some black pepper and cook for a few more minutes. Add the tuna and combine gently so that the tuna doesn't disintegrate too much.

5 When the pasta is cooked, add it to the frying pan and stir again to combine. Tip the mixture into a shallow ovenproof dish, spread out evenly and pour over the cheese sauce.

6 Sprinkle over the grated cheese and bake in the preheated oven for 20–25 minutes or until the cheese is golden.

Variations

- If you have no cheese sauce or for a lighter bake, just pile the pasta mix into the dish, top with the grated cheese (using extra for better coverage) and bake without the sauce.

- You can use bacon or chicken pieces instead of the tuna – cook these in the oil with the onion. You can use fresh tuna – again, chop and cook in the oil for 2 minutes with the onion.

- To make it more interesting, you can add a small amount of red wine to the sauce (the alcohol boils away). You can also add a tbsp of half-fat crème fraîche to make it really creamy. A spoonful of red pesto sauce (not for nut allergy sufferers) makes the tomato sauce taste richer too.

- Stir in sweetcorn before putting it into the oven dish to make it extra tasty.

Meat lasagne

Serves 6 children

Suitable for ages 9 months +

❄ **Will freeze (best frozen before baking)**

Nutrition ⬤ Fat ⬤ Saturates ⬤ Sugar ⬤ Salt

1 quantity bolognese sauce (see page 70)

1 quantity cheese sauce (see page 134)

8 sheets no pre-cook lasagne

2 tbsp freshly grated Parmesan

NUTRITION NOTES
Try to buy mince with 10% rather than 20% fat to reduce the fat and saturates content.

SERVING SUGGESTION
You can add salad and garlic bread to make it a feast!

1   Make up the two sauces if you haven't any in the freezer. Keep both warm. Preheat the oven to 180°C/350°F/Gas 4.

2   Thin the bolognese sauce down a little with 50ml water, mixing it in well (the pasta absorbs moisture, and if the sauce is too thick the pasta won't cook properly).

3   Spread a third of the bolognese sauce on the base of a four-serving lasagne dish and cover with a layer of lasagne sheets. You may have to break them to make them fit, don't overlap. Add another layer of bolognese and dribble half the cheese sauce on top followed by more dry lasagne, the rest of the bolognese, another layer of lasagne and finally the remaining cheese sauce and the grated cheese.

4   Bake in the preheated oven for 40 minutes or until bubbling and golden.

Variations
Add chopped mushrooms, finely chopped red pepper, aubergine or courgette to the bolognese sauce while cooking the onions, or add chopped mushrooms for the last minute of onion-cooking time.

Yummy vegetable lasagne

Serves 4 children

Suitable for ages 9 months +

❊ **Will freeze (best frozen before baking)**

Nutrition ⬤ Fat   ◑ Saturates   ◯ Sugar   ◑ Salt

*1 quantity roast vegetable sauce
(see below)*

*1 quantity cheese sauce (see
page 134)*

50ml milk

8 sheets of pre-cook lasagne

2 tbsp freshly grated Parmesan

NUTRITION NOTES

Plenty of fibre, carotenes, vitamin C and all sorts of goodies in here, and because it is meat free there are fewer saturates. The cheese sauce provides most of the protein.

1   Follow the method for meat lasagne on page 127, but using the roast vegetable sauce instead of the meat sauce.

2   Thin down the cheese sauce with the extra milk (beat it in with a wooden spoon until smooth). This is to ensure that there is enough moisture in the dish for the lasagne sheets to cook properly.

Variations

For a runnier mixture combine the vegetables with some quick tomato sauce (see page 76) or ready-made good-quality tomato sauce. For this version you can add some large fresh cloves of unpeeled garlic to the roasting pan and squeeze out their cooked flesh into the tomato sauce, stirring well.

Roast vegetable sauce

Sent in by Netmums member Priti: 'Cut up about 800g mixed Mediterranean vegetables – e.g. red pepper, courgette, aubergine and red onion – into smallish squares/cubes. Drizzle with 1–2 tbsp olive oil and a little seasoning, and roast at 190°C/375°F/Gas 5 for 40 minutes or until everything is soft, turning two or three times. Add tomatoes (cherry ones are especially good) halfway through, and halved chestnut mushrooms if you want. '

Pies

'There is something incredibly satisfying about taking a golden-topped gorgeous-smelling pie out of the oven. Even if it's just me and my two little ones. I grandly call "Stand back now, everyone" as I present it to the table using my oven gloves. I think I might even dig out my never-worn apron to complete my little scene of domestic bliss next time!' Claudia, mum to Sophia and Mia

If you want your children to wolf down their tea and ask for seconds, you won't go wrong if you serve them a steaming hot pie. If you've made it yourself, it'll disappear even more quickly! They'll think you're the best cook on the planet. And you'll feel a bit smug because you'll know how good for them it is. In fact most pies are very straightforward to make and so forgiving that even the least experienced parent can rustle them up. Knocking out your own pastry really does take only a couple of minutes but there are several delicious, even easier topping alternatives all of which, so our Netmums kids' empty plates tell us, are just as tasty. The pies we've chosen here are the old favourites plus a couple with a 'twist'. DO give them a go: as with many of the recipes in this book, they will freeze well so batch cooking will save you time another day.

Pie toppings

You'll find pies more suitable for eating cold or taking on picnics in other parts of this book. Here our pies are those best dished up on a cold winter evening in a cosy kitchen. Although some combinations are traditional (e.g. mash with mince in shepherd's pie or cottage pie/pastry with chunks of chicken in a creamy leek filling), you can mix and match most pie fillings with most kinds of topping. The only thing that doesn't really work is to cover a very liquid filling (e.g. the chicken and leek) with mash or crumble, as it will just sink into the filling and get 'lost'. Here's a run-down of the types of topping and what you might use them with:

Shortcrust pastry Great made with butter or a good-quality polyunsaturated margarine. Useful for any meat, poultry, vegetable or fish pie with a fairly liquid filling. Use a pie funnel to stop the pastry dipping in the filling. Use to top pie only – no need to do double crust. Needs a glaze of full-cream milk or beaten egg to look really good.

Continued

Puff pastry Good for same pies as shortcrust (needs glazing too) and is also great as a very easy, quick open pie – just roll out the pastry into a square, rectangle or round, neaten it up, score halfway through the pastry all the way round 3cm from the edge and then evenly distribute a quick topping, e.g. steamed chopped leeks and goat's cheese slices, or cooked Mediterranean vegetables and grated Cheddar, and bake until golden and bubbling. The outside edge rises up as it bakes and gives a raised edge to the tart.

Filo pastry Good if you're keeping an eye on the family's calorie or fat intake – the basic filo is very low in fat. Also quick as the filo comes in sheets that are ready to use. Just brush the slices with olive oil and use in layers (three to five is about right) to top your pie, finishing with a brushing of oil. Also brilliant filled with seasoned ricotta cheese and spinach purée bound with a beaten egg and rolled up into parcels before baking.

Mashed potato/other mash Number one low-cost easy topping. Ideal for less liquid fillings such as minced meat, fish pie. You don't have to pipe the potato on – just use a spatula or even a large shallow spoon to spread it gently over the top of the pie. Fluff up with a fork to make more crunchy bits. Potato mash can be mixed with other roots such as sweet potato, swede or parsnip for a change and varied nutrition.

Sliced potato Fairly thick slices of cooked potato brushed with a light olive oil or melted butter are great – go for a waxy old potato rather than a floury type such as King Edward – and even quicker than mash.

Crumble Savoury crumble is easy and looks great. It can be made simply with flour and butter, or with added rolled oats or with chopped nuts or even seeds (not for nut allergy sufferers).

Cobbler This is basically a scone pastry and you simply cut rounds out with a glass or cutter and place them on top of the pie, therefore quicker than making a traditional pie crust. Goes well with almost any filling as long as it isn't too liquid. See page 129.

TIP
You can, of course, use ready-made pastry from the chilled or frozen counter; we all use it sometimes. But it may contain hydrogenated fats (see page 25) and we think the flavour of home-made (especially using butter or part butter) is nicer.

A few words about pie fillings

Pies are a great chance to get vegetables into veggie-shy children. It seems that when the veg are soaked with delicious sauce and cut into small pieces, they are just fine. There is also great scope to purée veggies and actually make them part of the liquid – e.g. tomatoes, onions, mushrooms – for kids who can spot even a tiny chunk of veg from 100 metres.

The meat in your pie can also be bulked up with other low-cost nutritious proteins such as brown lentils (delicious, actually, if you've never given them a go), or chickpeas. Basically, as long as your total filling weights are more or less the same as those in the recipes that follow, you can make up the filling to suit yourself and what ingredients you have available. We've given you some ideas at the end of each recipe to get you started.

Very quick fish pie

Cathy from Harrow says: *'This is such an easy dish and goes down a storm with children. My kids like it made in individual pie dishes. They don't have a massive appetite so we use ramekin dishes.'*

Serves 3–4 children

Suitable for ages 6 months +

❋ Will freeze (best frozen before the final cooking). When defrosted, oven bake at 180°C/350°F/ Gas 4 for 30 minutes or until the centre is piping hot

Nutrition   ◖ Fat   ● Saturates   ◖ Sugar   ◖ Salt

400g haddock, cod or other white fish steak or fillet

500g waxy old potatoes

100g broccoli florets

1 quantity cheese sauce (see page 134)

25g Cheddar, freshly grated

NUTRITION NOTES
Bags of calcium and protein in this dish and, depending on what you add to it, can be a source of a variety of vitamins.

SERVING SUGGESTION
Great with green beans, broccoli, peas or even carrots. A light fruit dessert (e.g fruit salad) would round the meal off well.

1   Bake the fish in a covered ovenproof dish – this takes about 20 minutes at 180°C/350°F/Gas 4. Or steam over a pan of boiling water for 4–5 minutes, or microwave on medium-high on a covered plate for 4 minutes or so.

2   Peel the potatoes and cut into medium chunks, then boil them until just tender. Drain and slice into discs about 5mm thick. Meanwhile lightly cook the broccoli florets, drain and cut into tiny bite-size florets if necessary.

3   Flake the cooked fish and place in a pie dish, picking out any bones as you come across them. Spoon the broccoli on top of the fish and pour over the cheese sauce. Place the potato discs evenly over the mixture so it is all covered and sprinkle over the grated cheese.

4   Bake in the preheated oven at the same temperature as above for about 15 minutes or until the topping has turned golden and is a little crisp.

Variations

- If you feel like it, it adds flavour to the dish if you poach the fish in the milk for the cheese sauce first. This takes only about 5 minutes with the liquid just simmering. Remove the fish to a plate with a slotted spatula, strain the milk and use in the cheese sauce recipe.

- Various vegetables can be used in the pie instead of the broccoli – pre-cooked chopped leeks, leaf spinach, slightly thawed petits pois.

- Small peeled prawns can be added to the pie: use about 25g per 125g white fish.

- Salmon fillet makes a nice addition: replace half the white fish with the same weight of salmon.

- Sliced hard-boiled egg also tastes great. Use 2 small eggs in the recipe above and scatter the slices in amongst the fish before pouring the sauce over.

- Mashed potato can be used instead of the potato slices. Keep the mash quite firm, i.e. use a little less milk in the mashing than normal. Firm mash is easier to handle and shape, and goes brown quicker.

- Instead of a cheese sauce you could use parsley sauce: omit the cheese from the sauce and add 2 tbsp finely chopped parsley instead.

Cheese sauce

Makes enough for approx. 4 children's servings

Suitable for ages 6 months +

❄ **Will freeze in lidded container or strong sealed bag**

Nutrition   ● Fat   ● Saturates   ○ Sugar   ○ Salt

40g butter

1 heaped tbsp plain flour

550ml semi-skimmed milk, room
   temperature or warm*

75g (approx.) Cheddar, grated

NUTRITION NOTES
* You could use whole milk if preferred
for extra calories and fat, and for
children under two. For children over five
you can use skimmed milk.

SERVING SUGGESTION
Use in the fish pie above or in pasta
bakes, lasagne, or simply poured over a
piece of cooked fish.

1   Melt the butter in a saucepan over a medium heat and then
stir in the flour. Continue to stir over a medium-high heat for
a minute and allow to bubble (this removes any 'floury'
taste from the sauce).

2   Gradually add the milk a little at a time, stirring after each
addition until the sauce smooths up again and thickens.
Each time you add some more milk it takes about a minute
to re-thicken. The more milk you add each time, the longer it
will take but if you add too much in one go it may go lumpy.
A balloon whisk or wooden spoon is best for this.

3   When all the milk is in, bring the sauce to a simmer, stirring,
then add the cheese, and stir until it is melted in.

Shepherd's pie

Serves 4 children

Suitable for ages 6 months +

❄ **Will freeze (best frozen before final cooking). Defrost thoroughly and bake at 200°C/400°F/Gas 6 for 30–40 minutes or until the top is bubbling and golden**

Nutrition ▢ Fat ▢ Saturates ▢ Sugar ▢ Salt

500g lean minced lamb

1 large onion, peeled and finely chopped

4 medium carrots, chopped

2 garlic cloves, peeled and crushed (optional)

200ml lamb stock

1 x 200g can chopped tomatoes

1 tbsp Worcestershire sauce

1 tbsp tomato purée

1 tsp mixed herbs

750g old potatoes, peeled and cut into even chunks

25g butter

NUTRITION NOTES

Another great excuse to sneak lots of veggies into the kids' tea without them complaining!

While lamb mince can be very high in fat and saturated fat, if you choose lamb labelled 'extra lean' or 'low in fat' and allow any surplus fat to drain out as explained above, then the fat content isn't too bad.

1   Preheat the oven to 200°C/400°F/Gas 6.

2   Place the meat in a large non-stick frying pan and heat gently, stirring frequently, until the meat begins to brown. Drain off any fat that comes out of the meat into a dish (you can put this in the fridge to harden then bin it). Don't pour it down the sink as this could cause a blockage.

3   Add the onion, carrot and garlic and continue to cook for 10 minutes. Stir in the stock and tomatoes and bring to the boil. Add the Worcestershire sauce, tomato purée and herbs, cover the pan and simmer gently for 25 minutes, giving it the occasional stir.

4   Meanwhile cook the potatoes in boiling water until tender, then drain and mash, mixing in the butter.

5   Turn the meat into an ovenproof dish. Gently spoon on the mashed potato evenly and smooth over with a spatula. (Rough up a little with a fork for more crunch and a rustic look.)

6   Cook in the preheated oven for about 30 minutes until the potatoes are golden brown.

Continued

If you are using stock cubes, they are usually very high in salt, as is Worcestershire sauce, so you won't need any extra salt in this pie. If you want to get the salt content lower, buy a ready-made, chilled-counter lamb or beef stock or use a low-salt variety of stock cube or bouillon.

Variations

- Shepherd's pie is made with lamb (shepherds look after sheep!) but, of course, you can use other meat in your pie if you want. The proper name for a similar pie made with minced beef is cottage pie.

- Try adding 200g or so of baked beans in tomato sauce to the mixture and reduce the amount of meat a little. Mash the beans down slightly if you like before stirring into the meat mix at step 2. The beans add flavour and fibre and reduce the total fat/saturates content. And it brings the cost down! Cooked brown or Puy lentils are also a great addition.

- Use parsnips or mushrooms instead of the carrots.

- For a tasty, crispy topping add a little grated cheese over the mashed potato for the last 10 minutes of cooking time.

- You could use slices of potato (see fish pie, pages 132–3) instead of mash for a change.

- Mhairi from south-east Scotland uses a crumble mixture to top her shepherd's pie. See the beef and bean crumble on page 139.

Chicken and leek pie

Sent in by Donna from Aberdeen.

Serves 4 children

Suitable for ages 1 year +

✳ **Will freeze before baking**

Nutrition ⬤ Fat   ⬤ Saturates   ◯ Sugar   ◯ Salt

2 medium to large leeks

50g unsalted butter

3–4 medium skinless chicken
   breast fillets, cut into large bite-
   sized pieces

50g plain flour

300ml full-cream milk

150ml chicken stock

salt and pepper

500g packet ready-to-roll puff
   pastry

1 small egg, beaten

NUTRITION NOTES
This is quite a high-fat dish so serve
plenty of fat-free accompaniments and
follow with some fresh fruit.

SERVING SUGGESTION
Serve with boiled or mashed potatoes,
carrots and peas.

1 Clean the leeks if necessary and chop them into rounds
   about 1cm thick. Melt the butter over a medium heat, add
   the leeks and sauté for a few minutes. Add the chicken to
   the leeks and sauté for another few minutes.

2 Stir in the flour and over a medium low heat, combine the
   flour with the buttery juices until it thickens up and
   becomes smooth. Cook for another minute. Now begin
   adding the milk, stirring. Add it quite slowly and by the time
   it is all in you'll have a thick white sauce. Use a wooden
   spoon to stir as you do so. Add enough stock, stirring well,
   to thin the sauce down – it may take all 150ml or a little
   less. Taste the sauce and add a pinch of salt if liked, and
   some black pepper.

3 Tip the mixture into a shallow pie dish and leave to cool. If
   you have a pie funnel to put in the centre (to stop the
   pastry falling down into the sauce and getting soggy) so
   much the better: put it in the dish now.

4 Preheat the oven to 200ºC/400ºF/Gas 6.

5 Roll out the pastry roughly into the shape of the pie dish,
   making sure it is at least 20 per cent bigger than the dish,
   and then carefully move the pastry on to the top of the pie.
   Press it down on to the pie rim all the way round and cut off
   most of the overhanging pastry (the pastry will shrink as it
   cooks so don't cut it too tight). Make a hole in the centre
   with a knife. Decorate the pastry with the trimmings if you
   like, and then brush the top of the pie with the beaten egg.

6 Bake in the preheated oven for about 25 minutes or until
   the pastry is golden.

Variations

You can add chopped chives or parsley to the filling or use
mushrooms instead of the leeks. You can use turkey
instead of the chicken.

Sausage, bean and vegetable cobbler

'My little boy is going through a sausage phase at the moment, and this goes down a treat, as I'm managing to get veg in as well as just sausages!'
Melanie from Peterborough

Serves 4 children

Suitable for ages 1 year +

✳ **Will freeze**

Nutrition ⬤ Fat ⬤ Saturates ◯ Sugar ◯ Salt

---

8 sausages

1 medium onion, peeled and
 chopped

1 tbsp olive oil

500g mixed veg, fresh or frozen
 (e.g. carrots, peas, sweetcorn)

1–2 tsp dried mixed herbs

200ml water or vegetable stock

1 x 400g can baked beans in
 tomato sauce

COBBLER TOPPING

125g self-raising flour

75g mature Cheddar cheese,
 freshly grated

1 small egg, beaten

1 tbsp olive oil

60ml milk, plus extra for brushing

NUTRITION NOTE
Masses of dietary fibre in this dish and
if you use extra-lean sausages you can
bring down the total and saturated fat
levels.

SERVING SUGGESTION
Serve with boiled potatoes or mash and
a leafy green vegetable.

1 Preheat the grill to medium-hot, and the oven to 180°C/350°F/Gas 4.

2 Grill the sausages until browned all over then leave to cool. Once cool, slice into reasonable bite-size pieces.

3 Cook the onion in the olive oil in a non-stick frying pan over a medium heat until transparent and just turning golden, about 10 minutes.

4 Chop any of the vegetables as necessary, then add them to the pan with the herbs and water or stock and cook for 15 minutes.

5 To make the cobbler, put the flour and grated cheese into a bowl. Add the egg, oil and milk. Using a fork, mix to a dough. Flour your clean, dry work surface or board then roll out to 2cm thick and cut out into circles using a small glass.

6 Add the beans and sausages to the vegetables, give it all a good stir and place in an ovenproof dish. Arrange the cobbler shapes on top of the mixture and brush with milk.

7 Bake in the preheated oven for 20 minutes or until the cobbler topping is golden.

Beef and bean crumble

Sent in by Mhairi from south-east Scotland.

Serves 4 children

Suitable for ages 9 months +

❄ **Will freeze (best frozen before baking)**

Nutrition   ⬤ Fat   ⬤ Saturates   ⬤ Sugar   ⬤ Salt

---

1 tbsp olive oil

*1 medium onion, peeled and
  chopped*

*4 medium carrots, peeled and
  coarsely grated*

2 garlic cloves, peeled and crushed

450g lean minced beef

150ml beef stock

50g tomato purée

*1–2 tsp dried mixed herbs
  (optional)*

*1 x 400g can baked beans in
  tomato sauce*

CRUMBLE

75g rolled oats

30g plain flour

60g Cheddar cheese, freshly grated

30g butter, melted

NUTRITION NOTES
Lots of lovely goodies in this one –
including tons of carotenes, fibre, iron,
vitamin B group and various plant
chemicals.

SERVING SUGGESTION
Serve with baked potato and green
vegetables.

1   Preheat the oven to 200°C/400°F/Gas 6.

2   Heat the oil in a large non-stick frying pan and add the
    onion and carrot. Fry over a medium heat until the onion
    begins to soften, then add the garlic and fry for another
    minute. Add the beef and continue to fry until it is browned,
    about 3 minutes or so.

3   Next add the beef stock, tomato purée and herbs (if using),
    and simmer over a low heat for 10–15 minutes.

4   Meanwhile make the crumble by mixing the oats, flour and
    cheese together, then adding the melted butter.

5   Once most of the liquid has evaporated from the beef
    mixture add the baked beans and warm through. Tip the
    beef mixture into a suitable ovenproof dish and cover with
    the crumble mixture.

6   Cook in the preheated oven for 25–30 minutes or until the
    topping is light golden brown.

Casseroles and Stews

'I find Monday my most difficult day of the week so I almost always make a casserole at the weekend and pop it in the fridge for Monday night. It makes Mondays more bearable because I feel one step ahead all day. After a delicious, nutritious, stress-free hot meal I'm ready for a glass of wine, knowing that I beat the Monday blues once again!' Lee, mum to Liam and Jemma

While you can't whip up a stew in the time it takes the kids to unpack their schoolbags, get changed and arrive in the kitchen hungry, they are very useful in another way. If you can plan ahead just a bit, you can make your stew and either have it cooking very slowly all day (if you have a slow oven or worktop slow cooker) or you can cook it the day before and simply reheat it. You can even heat individual portions in the microwave. And of course stews are very adaptable — as long as you have more or less the right amount of liquid and don't cook them up too high, they will time and again produce a tasty meal with little fuss. You can also more or less invent the content to suit what you have available or what your family enjoys. Lastly, in the winter months they are the ideal health food, and a great way to add different vegetables to your child's diet. See opposite for tips on making your stews extra healthy.

In this section we have four gorgeous stews to try but first, if you're a stew virgin, read the panel on the basic method for most stews that you'll want to cook on page 142.

Stew or casserole?

What is the difference between a stew and a casserole? Well, a stew is generally something cooked on the hob in a large saucepan or stewpan, while a casserole is generally cooked in the oven. But the two are very interchangeable: you can make a stew and put it in the oven so it's a casserole; or you can take your favourite casserole recipe, put it on the hob to cook and it's a stew. Or it could be a hotpot!

It is up to you which way to cook the stews on these pages but if it is winter and you want the oven on, you may as well cook it in the oven as long as your casserole dish has a good, tight-fitting lid. This will save you having to check that the hob temperature is low enough and will avoid any chance of the bottom layer of stew burning (although a good-quality saucepan with a very heavy base will help prevent this). It is also a good idea to invest in one or two good-quality flameproof casserole dishes, as this means you can brown your veg and meat on the hob and then put the casserole in the oven without transferring the contents of the pan.

Making stews healthy

While some fat in the meat helps make the meat tender, try to avoid the fattiest cuts — and cut most of the visible fat off. Braising steak and neck of lamb are two ideal cuts.

There is no need to keep the skin on chicken in a stew. Chicken with its skin is higher in fat and saturated fat than beef!

Add plenty of vegetables. Try to get a mix of roots (e.g. carrots, swede) and green veg (e.g. cabbage, beans) for a British-style stew or go for plenty of Mediterranean veggies for a more exotic feel!

Add pulses. Lentils are easily and quickly cooked within the stew. Unless you are prepared to soak overnight and fast boil, you are better off adding canned ready-cooked red kidney beans, borlottis etc. to the stew. Pulses are rich in soluble fibres and a good source of protein.

When you have finished cooking the stew, if you can see shiny fat on the top then let it cool and spoon off with a fairly flat large spoon, or if possible cool in the fridge overnight and then remove the solidified fat by hand.

Basic stew method

1   Heat some oil in your stewpan or flameproof casserole dish on the hob and add your chunks of meat and brown for a few minutes over a high heat, removing the pieces once they are brown on to a plate. Browning the meat adds flavour and colour but don't over-brown as charred meat tends to be tough.

2   Now turn the heat down, add a little more oil and your chopped onion. Most stews do contain onion as it adds depth of flavour, aroma, richness and sweetness. Stir it around to soften and brown slightly and if you're adding garlic or spices do so now and stir them around well for a minute.

3   Add the meat and the rest of your suitable chopped vegetables back into the pan, and stir. At this point you can add some flour to thicken the stew, stirring it in well, if the recipe requires it (see Box page 144).

4   Now add your liquid and herbs. Stir well and bring to a simmer on medium-high. Once your simmer has been reached, turn the heat down low and check a few minutes later to make sure it is still simmering. Put the lid on and leave to cook for the length of time the recipe specifies. At this stage if you are slow-cooking, transfer to your slow oven.

5   Check once or twice during cooking that the stew isn't bubbling too fast, or too slow, and check that the liquid isn't disappearing. If it is, add a little water and stir.

6   Before serving the stew check a piece of meat (if using) and veg to make sure they are tender, and check the seasoning.

THICKENERS

There are various ways to thicken the liquid in a stew. You generally want the finished liquid to be much less runny than, say, a thin soup and you want it full of flavour. If it is too thin it will taste thin too.

Early flour method Traditionally the pieces of meat are coated in seasoned flour and then browned. This method is a bit hit and miss as, if you brown the meat properly the flour may burn and it won't thicken the liquid properly. So add the flour once the meat has browned (see below). Generally you need 1 level tbsp plain flour for a stew to serve four people. You need to make sure the flour is cooked in the fat in the pan before adding the liquid.

Late flour method If you find the stew a bit thin and it is near serving time, you can thicken it quickly by mixing together a knob of butter and some plain flour in a dish and then add a little of the cooking liquid to the butter-flour mix and blend it well. Add a bit more and when the mix is just about runny, you can pour it back into the stew pan, stir well and bubble for a few minutes, to thicken the whole stew. (If you want to cheat, use thickening granules.)

Carbohydrates method Floury old potatoes and some soft pulses such as cooked butter beans and red lentils are ideal as stew thickeners: either cook them in the stew and then roughly mash them down with a fork, or you can cook some separately, mash and add to the pan later. Or you can add small pasta shapes any time up to the last 20 minutes or so of cooking time, which will absorb liquid and thicken the stew up nicely.

Tomato purée method Tomato paste, purée or even tomato sauce in jars can be used to thicken the stew slightly. This needs to be added near the start or, at least, well before cooking is finished to avoid a slightly tart flavour.

Lid off/long cooking method If you can see that your stew is too runny and the liquid looks thin and is lacking flavour, you need to reduce the amount of liquid by allowing the dish to cook without the lid and perhaps by increasing the temperature slightly. This is best done on the hob. Stir frequently to get more steam out.

Blender method If your stew contains just meat and non-carb veg such as carrots, onions and greens, it may end up a bit thin and weedy by the end of cooking time especially if you added too much liquid. If you have no time to mess about, don't panic. The way to get it thickened without adding extra items to the stew (e.g. late flour or carbs method) is to remove some (about a quarter) of the finished stew to a blender, blend it up and return the blended portion to the pan, stir it in well and reheat. This will also add flavour to the liquid.

TIP
Stews left overnight and reheated will almost always thicken up, especially if there are carbs such as potatoes, pasta or pulses in the dish.

Simple chicken stew

This is based on a recipe sent in by Victoria from North Lincs, who says: *'I have just made a fantastic stew and thought I would pass it on to you guys! It is great as you can use any veg you like and it makes a very wholesome family meal and a great way to make your kids eat veg. You can use chicken breast or leg portions or you can use up the leftover chicken from the Sunday roast.'*

Serves 4 children

Suitable for ages 9 months +

❊ **Will freeze. Best frozen when slightly undercooked, finish cooking on reheating**

Nutrition ◯ Fat ◯ Saturates ◯ Sugar ◯ Salt

---

1 tbsp olive oil

4 chicken portions, most of the fat removed (see Variations)

1 large onion, peeled and chopped

2 large carrots, peeled and chopped

4 medium old potatoes, peeled and quartered

1–2 parsnips, peeled and chopped

450ml chicken stock

1–2 tsp mixed herbs

NUTRITION NOTES

Chicken stew is traditional cold-weather, cold-prevention, cure-all fare. Apparently it is because of all the goodness in the chicken bones!

SERVING SUGGESTION

You could serve with some chunky crusty bread to dip into the gravy.

1   Heat the oil in a heavy-based lidded stewpan and cook the chicken pieces over a high heat for a few minutes, turning, until white and tinged golden.

2   Remove the chicken from the pan on to a plate while you cook the onion in the same oil and pan over a medium heat until soft.

3   Add the rest of the ingredients including the chicken to the pan, stir well and bring to a simmer. Put the lid on and leave to simmer on a low heat for $1\frac{1}{2}$ hours.

4   Mash a couple of the pieces of potato down to thicken the gravy a little, and serve straight to the table.

Variations

Parsnips are very sweet in a stew so you could use swede instead. You could add a tbsp of tomato purée. You could tip in some sliced green beans or peas for a bit of greenery. You can make the stew thicker using any of the methods outlined in the Box opposite.

You can cut up a small whole chicken and use instead of the portions. Chicken with the bone left in produces the tastiest and most tender stew, as the bones contain marrow and other goodies. Chicken breast portions are less successful in a stew than leg meat as they tend to dry out. If using bone-in meat you can always remove the bone before serving for young children.

You can use leftover chicken, but just add it with the vegetables, don't cook it in the oil.

Beef stew and dumplings

From Sonia from Lancashire, who says: *'If your children turn their noses up at this one then ask them to dip some crusty buttered bread in the gravy and try it – it's so tasty they won't be able to resist!'*

1 tbsp olive oil

500g stewing or braising steak
  (cut up into very small cubes if
  your children are not used to big
  chunks of meat)

1 large onion, peeled and chopped

1 garlic clove, peeled and chopped

1 tbsp plain flour

500ml beef stock

1 tbsp tomato purée

3 medium carrots, peeled and
  chopped

1 tbsp balsamic vinegar

DUMPLINGS

175g self-raising flour

75g shredded suet

1 tbsp finely chopped parsley

a good pinch each of salt and
  pepper

water, to mix

NUTRITION NOTES

You could serve with a green vegetable or even add the veg to the stew – for instance, white cabbage goes well here. This would add more vitamin C and plant chemicals to the dish. Beef is rich in iron, which is more easily absorbed with plenty of vitamin C.

SERVING SUGGESTION

Serve with mashed or boiled potatoes to soak up the gravy or with bread.

Serves 4 children

Suitable for ages 9 months +

❄ **Will freeze. Best frozen partially cooked, then cooked through after thawing**

Nutrition ⬭ Fat ⬭ Saturates ⬭ Sugar ⬭ Salt

1   Preheat the oven to 170°C/325°F/Gas 3.

2   In a large flameproof lidded casserole, heat the oil and fry the meat over a high heat, turning until brown on all sides. Remove to a plate and then turn the heat down a little. Add the onion (and a little more oil if necessary) and cook until it is translucent. Add the garlic and stir in the flour thoroughly. Add the stock, tomato purée, carrots and balsamic vinegar.

3   Cover with a tightly fitting lid and place in the preheated oven for around 2 hours. Braising steak tends to get more tender the longer you cook it. Check halfway through to make sure it is cooking gently.

4   Meanwhile, make the dumplings. Sieve the flour into a bowl and add the suet, parsley, salt and pepper. Add enough water to make a soft but not sticky dough, around 2–3 tbsp. Lightly flour your hands and roll the dough into eight small balls.

5   Add the dumplings to the stew 20 minutes before the end of cooking time and check to make sure there is enough liquid as the dumplings absorb liquid and their outer coating of flour thickens the stew.

6   Add salt and pepper if necessary before serving, but you should find that the stock gives enough seasoning.

Sweet sausage casserole

Sent in by Amanda, who says: 'This is *a recipe I made up*, desperate as usual to get my children to eat vegetables! The butternut squash will *disintegrate* and so may the sweet potato, so there's *two vegetables* your children don't know they're eating!'

1 tbsp olive oil

1 medium red (or white) onion, peeled and chopped

8 good-quality sausages, cut into chunks

1 large red eating apple

1 medium sweet potato, peeled and diced

1 small or ½ large butternut squash, peeled and diced

1 large carrot, peeled and diced

1 x 400g can chopped tomatoes

1 chicken stock cube, crumbled

1 dsp tomato chutney or paste

salt and pepper

a little hot water

NUTRITION NOTES

Yes, this is certainly an orange veggie feast – tons of beta-carotene here and it's full of fibre and vitamin E. Go for high pork meat (or beef) butcher's sausages rather than cheap ones if possible as they contain much less fat.

SERVING SUGGESTION

You can serve with a side salad, or peas or green beans.

Serves 4 children

Suitable for ages 9 months +

✳ **Will freeze. Best frozen partially cooked, then cook through after defrosting**

Nutrition   ◖ Fat   ◖ Saturates   ◯ Sugar   ◖ Salt

1 Preheat the oven to 170°C/325°F/Gas 3.

2 Heat the oil in a flameproof casserole and over a medium heat cook the onion until transparent, about 8 minutes. Then chuck the sausages in the pan with the onions and brown gently for a further 8 minutes until lightly browned.

3 While the sausages are cooking, slice and core the apple (don't worry about peeling – and you may have space for 2 apples). When the sausages are ready add the apple slices to the pan with all the vegetables, and finally the rest of the ingredients (but don't season) and a dash of hot water.

4 Stir well, bring to a simmer, put the lid on and cook for an hour, then turn the heat down to 150°C/300°F/Gas 2 and cook for another 30–60 minutes. Check the dish two or three times. Alternatively you could cook on the hob, checking from time to time that the food isn't sticking.

5 The finished casserole is quite thick rather than runny, but if it is looking too dry add a dash of water when you check. Check seasoning before serving.

Variations

You can add a few sliced mushrooms to the casserole. Vegetarians could use veggie sausages.

Vegetable and bean pot

Serves 4 children

Suitable for ages 1 year +

※ **Will freeze. Best frozen partially cooked, then cook through after defrosting**

Nutrition ⬭ Fat   ⬭ Saturates   ⬭ Sugar   ⬭ Salt

1 tbsp light olive oil

1 medium onion, peeled and finely chopped

1 garlic clove, peeled and well crushed

1 medium sweet potato, peeled and cut into small cubes

1 medium parsnip, peeled and cut into small cubes

100g cabbage, shredded

200g canned chopped tomatoes

100ml vegetable stock

1 x 200g can butter beans, drained and rinsed

1 x 400g can green lentils, drained and rinsed

1   Heat the oil in a flameproof lidded pan and sauté the onion over a medium heat until soft and transparent, about 8 minutes. Add the garlic clove for the last minute or two of cooking time.

2   Add the sweet potato and parsnip and stir for a minute or two, then add the remaining ingredients, stir and bring to a simmer. Turn the heat down, put the lid on and simmer for 40–50 minutes or until everything is tender – or transfer to the oven to cook for the same length of time at 180°C/350°F/Gas 4.

3   Add extra stock or hot water if the mix begins to look too dry towards the end of cooking.

Variations

Cannellini beans can be used instead of the butter beans, or you could use a can of mixed pulses instead of the lentils. Sliced red or yellow pepper can be added with the onion.

NUTRITION NOTES

The casserole is a good source of protein, complex carbohydrate, carotenoids, B1, B3, folate, vitamin E, potassium and iron. It is an excellent winter meal, although quite low in calories. For extra protein and calories you can grate 1 tbsp hard cheese over each serving, which will add calcium too.

SERVING SUGGESTION

This is a complete meal but you can serve with crusty bread.

Spicy

'I was actually amazed *when my children started taking tastes of our Indian takeaway and asking for more. So* I started experimenting *with adding spices to their food –* and they loved it*! I've since been told that as children have underdeveloped taste-buds, they do enjoy mild to* medium spices*. It makes food so much more* interesting for them *and it helps them develop a taste for varied foods which helps* cut out fussiness*.'* Crissy, mum to Isabelle, Aimee and Ethan

Most adults think that children – especially small children – won't like spiced food, that it will be too hot or too unusual for them to enjoy. However, children do seem to have a taste for spices. While they may not be able to eat a vindaloo, they will happily eat a medium chilli con carne or a spiced soup or mild curry. It's all a matter of degree. If you're sensible, the adults don't have to give up their curries at family mealtime.

Tips for adding spices to children's meals

- Ground dry spices (including curry powders) stored for more than a few weeks (especially in a hot, light kitchen) will lose their flavour and aroma. Discard! Curry pastes in jars keep their characteristics better for longer, especially if stored in the fridge. If you can be bothered, buy whole spices and a little electric grinder and grind them when you need them for best flavour.

- Choose mild fresh chillies rather than dried ones.

- Always seed chillies as the seeds are the hottest part by far. The flesh of the jalapeño types is mild and pleasant.

- Ready chillies in jars can be quite hot so go easy when adding these.

- Liquid chilli in small bottles can be hottest of all – and can taste quite raw so be careful.

- Cumin and coriander seed are two very tasty mild and warm spices and most children will enjoy meals that include these. Saffron and cinnamon are two others.

- Garam masala is a spice mix that children like, containing cumin, coriander, cardamom and black pepper (and sometimes other additions such as ginger). It is usually added towards the end of cooking time rather than with the onion.

- When cooking meals with spice, add the ground spice or spice paste at the end of onion cooking time (i.e. if onions are fried in oil at the start of the recipe). The frying releases their aromas and flavour and helps take off any rawness.

- The more regularly people eat spicy foods the more 'immune' they get to the heat – and that applies to children as much as adults.

- Dairy items such as natural yoghurt, fromage frais or soured cream, and coconut milk cool down spicy dishes, so have plenty of one of those on tap to go with a spicy meal.

Mild chicken curry

1¹/₂ tbsp light olive oil

1 medium onion, peeled and finely chopped

150g broccoli, cut into small florets

2 garlic cloves, peeled and chopped

1–2 mild chillies, seeded and finely chopped, or ¹/₂ tsp ground chilli powder

1 tsp ground coriander

1 tsp ground cumin

¹/₂ tsp ground turmeric or saffron

black pepper

4 boneless chicken pieces, skinned and cut into bite-size cubes

100ml chicken stock

1 x 400g can chopped tomatoes

1 small bunch coriander leaves

NUTRITION NOTES

A child-friendly mild curry is another great way to add some vegetables to their supper. As spices are very good for health in several ways, it is a good idea to get children introduced to them early in life. They also cut down on the need for salt as a flavour enhancer.

SERVING SUGGESTION

Boiled basmati rice and plenty of natural yoghurt. You can add chopped cucumber to the yoghurt if you like for a raita.

Serves 4 children

Suitable for ages 1 year +

❋ **Will freeze**

Nutrition ◗ Fat ◗ Saturates ◗ Sugar ◗ Salt

1   Heat the oil in a large non-stick lidded frying pan and sauté the onion over a medium heat until transparent; about 8 minutes. Meanwhile parboil the broccoli florets for 3 minutes, and drain.

2   Add the garlic and all the spices to the onion pan and stir for a minute or two until the spices are full of aroma. Add the chicken pieces and stir over the heat for a few minutes to colour.

3   Add the broccoli, stock and tomatoes, stir well, bring to simmer and put the lid on. Cook for 20–30 minutes or until the chicken is cooked through and you have a rich sauce.

4   Serve garnished with coriander leaves.

Variations

- If you want a slightly quicker recipe you can omit the chillies, coriander, cumin, turmeric and pepper and instead add 1–2 dsp of a mild curry paste or dry mix.

- You can stir the yoghurt into the curry before serving if you prefer.

- Alter the vegetables according to what you have or like. You can omit the vegetables (not the canned tomatoes) if you like and instead serve a side salad.

- You can use turkey, beef or lamb instead of the chicken, of course. Red meats can take stronger spices than chicken.

- You can curry prawns, crab or firm white fish if you like – they take less cooking than meats and vegetables.

- For a vegetarian curry, use a selection of firm vegetables such as sweet potato (very nice), squash, cauliflower and potato instead of the meat. To save time you can parboil roots for 8 minutes and other veg for 3 minutes before adding them to the onions and frying for a minute or two.

Chilli con carne

Sent in by Lena from Edinburgh, who says: *'If you are making this for your children for the first time, just add a little chilli powder and cumin. Serve their portion and then spice the rest of the mixture up for the adults.'*

Serves 4 children

Suitable for ages 1 year +

※ **Will freeze**

Nutrition ◯ Fat ◯ Saturates ◯ Sugar ◯ Salt

---

1 tbsp olive oil

1 medium onion, peeled and finely chopped

1 garlic clove, peeled and chopped

400g lean beef or turkey mince

1 x 400g can tomatoes

1 tsp chilli powder (or more/less to taste)

$1/2$ tsp ground cumin

black pepper

1 x 400g can kidney beans (or mixed beans if preferred), drained and rinsed

NUTRITION NOTES

This is a very healthy supper – quite low in fat and salt, and full of vitamins, minerals, fibre and vitamin C.

SERVING SUGGESTION

Boiled rice or garlic bread or baked potatoes and side salad.

1 Heat the oil in a large saucepan and fry the onion over a medium heat for a few minutes until soft. Add the garlic and fry for another minute.

2 Put in the mince, turn the heat up a little and cook until lightly browned. Add the tomatoes, chilli powder, cumin and pepper. Bring to the boil and simmer for 30 minutes, stirring occasionally.

3 Then put in the kidney beans, and simmer for 15–20 minutes, stirring occasionally.

Variations

Add 1 large green pepper, seeded and finely chopped, to the onion in the pan at the start of the cooking time. For a richer depth of flavour, add 1 tbsp sun-dried tomato purée or red pesto (pesto sauces usually contain pine nuts or other nuts, so avoid for children allergic to nuts) to the dish at end of step 2. Instead of chilli powder, add 2 (more or less to taste) fresh seeded finely chopped red chillies. (Jalapeños are quite mild while Scotch Bonnet or the very small, thin type are much hotter.) Or you can add 1–2 tsp ready-minced chilli from a jar.

More spicy ideas

- Use a pinch of saffron or turmeric to colour and spice up boiled rice.

- Use fresh, finely chopped ginger and chilli in stir-fries to give added interest.

- Put a stick of cinnamon in stewed fruit – you will need less added sugar this way.

- Add $^1/_2$–1 tsp garam masala to casseroles, savoury pie fillings, etc., a few minutes before the end of cooking time to add warmth in winter.

- For risottos, add $^1/_2$ tsp of paprika, cumin powder or cinnamon when sautéing onions to give your final dish more taste without being too spicy.

- For more flavour in your eggy bread, add a little cinnamon to the beaten egg and milk mixture before soaking the bread in it (see page 81).

- Pour boiling water over a little grated fresh root ginger, add some lemon juice and honey, and you have a comforting hot drink, good for colds.

Lunch and picnic boxes

For most mums, packed lunches seem to represent years of sighing over the sliced bread and trying to think of variations on basic cheese or ham sandwiches that will actually get eaten, along with a vaguely healthy treat to brighten their day. Add to this the fact that you also want to provide a healthy balanced meal that will keep their physical and, mental energy levels up until home-time and, suddenly, chucking a few items of food into a lunchbox takes on a whole new importance.

Hopefully, some of the recipes and ideas in this chapter will help give you some good ideas, while Chapter 3 offers plenty of simple ideas for well-balanced lunches at home. For a week's worth of lunchbox ideas, see page 42.

These recipes can all also be used for picnics, days out and travelling. When out and about, it's much nicer for the kids to have some food and snacks prepared at home, rather than having to buy high-fat, high-salt, not-so-nice meals from expensive cafés.

Three Dips with Crudités

'Dips and crudités are a winner for school lunches, afternoon snacks or for that hour before tea when everyone needs something to keep them going. Making up the dips is a good one for "cooking" with little people as it's quick and easy and they can't do it too much damage!'
Nicola, mum to James

Serves each dip will serve 6–8 people, depending on what else is on offer!

Suitable for ages 1 year +

Hummus

Netmums member, Lisa, says: 'My girls' favourite starter is dips with veg sticks/crudités, bread sticks and pitta bread. If I'm in a real hurry, I use bought hummus mixed with plain/Greek-style yoghurt.'

1 x 400g can chickpeas, rinsed and drained

2 tbsp water or vegetable stock

1 garlic clove, peeled and roughly chopped

2 tbsp tahini (sesame seed paste, see Tip)

2 tbsp lemon juice

black pepper

chopped parsley to taste (optional)

2 tbsp olive oil

3 tbsp plain/Greek-style yoghurt

NUTRITION NOTES
If your child has a seed allergy omit the tahini.

TIP
You can use a pestle and mortar to blend up this dip if you prefer.

Nutrition ◗ Fat ◗ Saturates ◗ Sugar ◗ Salt

1 Put the chickpeas and the stock or water in a food processor, and blend for 30 seconds.

2 Add the garlic, tahini and lemon juice, black pepper and parsley (if using), and blend again.

3 Add the olive oil and yoghurt and blend again until the hummus is fairly smooth.

Cream cheese dip

1 x 200g carton cream cheese

200ml natural or Greek yoghurt

chopped chives to taste (optional)

Nutrition  Fat ⬤ Saturates ◯ Sugar ◯ Salt

1　Mix the cream cheese with the yoghurt until smooth.

2　Add the chives if using.

Soured cream and corn dip

100ml soured cream

100ml mayonnaise

50g Cheddar cheese, grated on the
　fine grater

3–4 tbsp cooked sweetcorn
　kernels

Nutrition ◯ Fat ◯ Saturates ◯ Sugar ◯ Salt

1　Mix all the ingredients together and serve.

Variations

Both the cream cheese and the soured cream dips can be varied by adding 1–2 tsp Dijon mustard or a dash of chilli sauce (but younger children may not be keen on either). For young ones try a tbsp tomato ketchup!

NUTRITION NOTES

Most dips are high in fat and these are no exception. But the hummus is a great source of vitamin E and fibre, and using natural low-fat yoghurt will bring the total and saturated fat content down, while the cream cheese and soured cream dips contain a little calcium. All the dips contain some protein.

SERVING SUGGESTION

Serve the dips with veg sticks/crudités, bread sticks and pitta bread slices or even some good-quality crisps (see home-made vegetable crisps on page 174). To make crudités, simply cut very fresh vegetables (washed and peeled as necessary) into batons about 6cm long and 5mm wide. Good veggies to use are carrots, celery, sweet peppers, spring onions and cucumber. You can also serve cherry tomatoes.

TIP

If you cut right back on – or even omit – the 'runnier' items in most home-made dips you can turn them into sandwich fillings. For example, use just a quarter the amount of soured cream and mayo in the corn dip and a quarter the amount of yoghurt in the cream cheese dip. A hummus spread can be made in a pestle and mortar by bashing chickpeas with just garlic, lemon juice, black pepper and olive oil.

Two sandwich fillings

These are much more nutritious than the fillings you can buy in little jars – and if you make a batch and freeze them it works out much lower in cost.

Lentil pâté

Makes enough for around 4 sandwiches

✳ **Will freeze**

Nutrition   ⬤ Fat   ⬤ Saturates   ⬤ Sugar   ⬤ Salt

100g mushrooms, finely chopped

1 clove garlic, peeled and well crushed

1 knob butter, about 30g

half a 400g can brown, green or red lentils, well drained

2 tbsp finely chopped parsley

black pepper

dash sea salt

juice from ¼ lemon (or dash vinegar)

NUTRITION NOTES
Brown and green lentils have more iron, B vitamins and selenium than red ones.

1 Fry the mushrooms and garlic over medium heat in the butter for a few minutes until soft.

2 Using a potato masher, pestle and mortar or fork, roughly mash the lentils and add them to the pan.

3 Add the parsley, pepper, salt and lemon juice (or vinegar) and stir well.

4 Spoon into a lidded container, press down with the back of a spoon, and chill.

Variations
For children who don't like mushrooms, very finely chop a small onion and fry instead of the mushrooms.

For a smoother pâté, if you have an extra couple of minutes, tip the cooked vegetables/lentils into the blender and blend for a minute; spoon out and chill.

Almost instant tuna spread

Makes enough for around 4 sandwiches

✳ **Will freeze**

Nutrition ▢ Fat   ▢ Saturates   ▢ Sugar   ▢ Salt

1 x 200g can tuna in springwater,
well drained

2 tbsp natural full-fat fromage
frais

1 tbsp light mayonnaise

dash lemon juice

black pepper

dash sea salt

NUTRITION NOTES
Whilst canned tuna doesn't contain
much omega-3 fat it is a good source of
protein, selenium and B and D vitamins.

1   Tip all the ingredients into a bowl, mix thoroughly, cover and
chill.

Variation

For older children you can add a couple of dashes of
Tabasco or other chilli sauce.

Wraps and Pittas

Wraps and pittas tick all the lunch and picnic needs boxes. They are quick to do, easy to do, adaptable, full of flavour, easy to eat, fun to eat and make a brilliant change from the usual sandwiches. No wonder parents and kids just love them!

IT'S A WRAP!

What is a wrap? It is a thin flour pancake that can be eaten hot or cold. The Mexican wrap is called a tortilla and was traditionally made with corn or maize flour but most supermarket wraps these days are wheat-flour based. Chinese spring roll wrappers are a similar idea though these are made with rice flour and are much thinner.

Want to make your own wraps? While bought wraps are fine, if you have the time or inclination you could try making your own. The basic mix is 225g fine corn or maize flour or wheat flour (or a mix of both), which are produced specifically for use in breads, 1 medium egg and a little warm water. Mix all together to a dough, knead until smooth and allow to stand for 30 minutes. Cut into 8 pieces, and roll these out very thinly to 8 pancakes. Griddle or dry-fry on a hot pan for a minute a side until speckled brown.

How to roll up a wrap Just pop a small amount of your wrap filling along the centre of your wrap from left to right. Fold up the right-hand side of the wrap so that it comes about a third of the way along your filling. Now starting nearest your body roll the wrap up so you have open filling at the left and a closed base at the right so the filling won't fall out when you eat it!

WRAP FILLING IDEAS

Fillings can be as simple or as innovative as you like; basically, you can use anything that will stay wrapped. You can also use hot wrap fillings which can be just as nice cold.

- Canned fish (e.g. salmon, tuna, preferably in water, otherwise use canned in oil), well drained and mixed with mayo or tomato sauce, plus salad items of choice e.g. tomato, cress, sweetcorn.

- Grated or thinly sliced cheese (e.g. Cheddar, mozzarella, soft mild goat's cheese, Emmental) with coleslaw and cherry tomatoes.

- Cooked sliced chipolatas or veggie sausages, hard-boiled egg, mayo mixed with tomato ketchup, crisp lettuce.

- Use the chicken satay recipe (see page 93), and add the chicken satay cubes to the wrap/pitta with chopped crunchy veg and a dressing made from natural yoghurt half and half with satay sauce or peanut butter.

- Roast some veggies (see page 128), allow to cool a little and toss with small cubes of halloumi or mozzarella or grated hard cheese and a dash of French dressing or olive oil and balsamic.

- Lightly crushed cooked (canned) chickpeas, chopped peppers, tomato and spring onion all tossed in hummus thinned with a little olive oil and lemon juice.

- Marinate Quorn chunks in light soy sauce for a few minutes, stir-fry and use instead of meat in your filling for a low-fat vegetarian alternative.

TIPS

For a party, pile some tortillas up on a plate, or some mini pittas. Put out a selection of fillings and filling ingredients, all chopped/diced/mixed as necessary, plus 3–4 dressings. Let them make up their own wraps/pitta pockets.

For easy eating, the lower half of the wrap or pitta can be encased in foil.

Transport, filling side up, in a deep lidded container, making sure the wraps/pittas are tucked in firmly so they don't fall over.

One wrap or pitta in a lunch box can be made spillproof by encasing firmly in clingfilm.

Wholemeal or white pitta? Wholemeal contains more fibre and B vitamins while white contains more calcium. If you serve pittas frequently, vary between white and wholemeal.

Wraps made from corn contain a reasonable amount of iron and are a good source of energy and carbohydrate. Wheat-based wraps have a similar nutrient content to white bread (if white flour is used) or wholemeal bread (if wholewheat flour is used). The label should have accurate nutrition information.

Cheesey beany wrap

Makes Approx. enough for 4 large wraps or pittas, or 6–8 small wraps or mini pittas

Suitable for ages 1 year +

Nutrition   ◖ Fat   ◖ Saturates   ◯ Sugar   ◖ Salt

1–2 tbsp groundnut oil or sunflower oil

1 red onion (about 100g), peeled and chopped

1 green pepper, seeded and chopped

3 tbsp cooked (or canned drained) red kidney beans, lightly mashed

3 tbsp cooked (or canned drained) sweetcorn kernels

50g Cheddar cheese, freshly grated

50g Emmental cheese, thinly sliced

1   Heat the oil in a non-stick frying pan, add the onion and pepper, and stir-fry for a few minutes over a medium-high heat to soften.

2   Add the kidney beans and stir for another few minutes, then take off the heat and allow to cool in a bowl.

3   Add the sweetcorn and cheeses to the bowl and stir.

Variations

You can add some mild or spicy tomato salsa when you make up the wrap/pitta, or a blob of mayo. You can add some finely chopped cooked lean beef or ham as well if you like. The vegetables can be cooked with some chopped garlic (add at kidney bean stage.)

Chicken and bacon wrap

Makes Approx. enough for 4 large wraps or pittas, or 6–8 small wraps or mini pittas

Suitable for ages 1 year +

Nutrition   ⬤ Fat   ◗ Saturates   ◗ Sugar   ◗ Salt

1 dsp olive oil

300g chicken fillet, diced

2 slices unsmoked lean back bacon, diced

1 tbsp mild tomato salsa

1 small ripe avocado

1 tbsp light mayonnaise

about 12 crisp lettuce leaves, shredded

1   Heat the oil in a non-stick frying pan and sauté the chicken and bacon until everything is cooked, stirring frequently. This will take about 4–5 minutes. Allow to cool.

2   Add the tomato salsa to a bowl and peel, stone and mash the avocado into it with the mayonnaise. Add the chicken and bacon and stir to combine.

3   Add the shredded lettuce to the pitta or wrap, top with the mixture and serve.

Variations

For kids who don't like avocado, omit and add 1 tbsp extra mayonnaise instead. For kids who don't like tomato salsa or avocado, add some mango chutney to the mayo.

Pastry Things

Whilst pastry can be high in fat and the ready-made kind is often high in trans fats, there is no harm in the kids having home-made pastry treats now and then, especially if they are burning off a lot of energy in sports and games.

Shortcrust pastry

Makes 350g, to serve 4–8 depending on recipe

Suitable for ages 1 year +

Will freeze before cooking

Nutrition   ● Fat   ● Saturates   ○ Sugar   ◐ Salt

250g plain flour

a pinch of salt

100g cold butter, cut into small cubes

5–6 tbsp cold water

NUTRITION NOTES

While shortcrust pastry is high in fat, if you make it yourself using good-quality butter it will contain no trans fats. You could also use half wholemeal flour to plain white flour, to increase the fibre content. This makes a 'nuttier' tasting pastry, which will be more crumbly and darker in colour.

TIP

If you have a food processor you can make pastry very easily. Put the flour, butter and salt in the food processor and pulse until the fat is combined with the flour. With the motor running, gradually add the water a very little at a time through the funnel until the dough comes together.

1   Put the flour and salt in a large mixing bowl and add the cubes of butter.

2   Working as quickly as you can, use your cool fingertips to rub the butter into the flour until you have a mixture that resembles coarse breadcrumbs.

3   Using a knife, stir in just enough of the cold water to bind the dough together.

4   Wrap the dough in clingfilm and chill in the fridge for 10–15 minutes before using in your recipe.

So-simple pizza pies

Recipe sent in by Lisa from Wolverhampton, who says: *'I made these with my kids. They are going through a fussy phase, and to my amazement, they ate them!'*

1 x 225g pack ready-made
   shortcrust pastry (or home-
   made, see page 165)

2 large eggs

150ml milk

a pinch of dried mixed herbs or
   1–2 tsp chopped fresh herbs of
   choice (eg parsley)

black pepper (optional)

5 tbsp freshly grated Cheddar

FILLING

your choice: e.g. canned/cooked
   sweetcorn, chopped peppers,
   chopped ham or chicken, sliced
   mushrooms, peas, whatever they
   will eat!

NUTRITION NOTES

These pies are a great way of getting the children to eat vegetables, are also a good source of calcium (in the cheese and milk), and contain some iron for the immune system and energy. Semi-skimmed milk rather than whole milk can be used for children over two. While the kids shouldn't eat pastry all day every day, if they're running round and burning up lots of calories, it is a good way to provide them with fuel. A lower-fat alternative would be to line the muffin tins with filo pastry instead.

SERVING SUGGESTIONS

These can be served hot with potato wedges (see page 104) and salad or veggies, or are good cold.

Serves 4 children

Suitable for ages 1 year +

✳ Will freeze at step 4 before baking

Nutrition ⬤ Fat ⬤ Saturates ◯ Sugar ◯ Salt

1 Preheat the oven to 180ºC/350ºF/Gas 4. Grease a four-hole muffin tray.

2 Get the children to help roll the pastry out until quite thin. Cut out four 10cm circles or rounds: small bowls do the job, or you could use a saucer. Line the muffin tray with the pastry circles.

3 Beat the eggs and milk together in a jug. Add the herbs and pepper (if liked). Get the children to put a bit of grated cheese in the bottom of each pastry case (leave 1 tbsp for sprinkling at the end). Then get them to add the fillings to each pie.

4 Pour on the egg/milk mixture until it nearly reaches the top of the pastry. Sprinkle with the remaining grated cheese. Carefully transfer to the preheated oven and bake for 20–25 minutes until lightly browned.

Variations

Using the same recipe ingredients, you can make a single quiche in a 20cm flan or pie tin, allowing an extra 5–10 minutes' cooking time.

Lisa says, *'Here are some other suggestions for fillings: sliced tomatoes, finely sliced leeks, flakes of tinned tuna, chopped spring onions, flaked salmon fillet.'*

Tuna parcels

Sent in by Justine, from Wyre, who says: *'Credit for this should go to our childminder.'*

Makes about 8 parcels

Suitable for ages 1 year +

❄ **Will freeze before baking**

Nutrition   ● Fat   ● Saturates   ○ Sugar   ◐ Salt

---

1 x 350g packet ready-made puff pastry (see Tip)

1 x 200g can tuna in spring water, well drained and flaked into a bowl

100g Cheddar, freshly grated

NUTRITION NOTES

Although there is a lot of fat in this recipe the cheese and tuna makes it a nutritious meal. Using tuna in water rather than brine reduces the salt content.

TIP

Puff pastry is quite time-consuming to make and if you only use it a few times a year it is okay to buy the bought stuff, whether frozen or from the chilled counter. Ready-made pastry may contain some trans fats so do check the labels.

1   Preheat the oven to 200°C/400°F/Gas 6.

2   Roll out the pastry as thinly as you can and cut into 8 squares.

3   Put some tuna and cheese in the middle, fold over into a triangle and go round the edges with a fork to seal (brushing the edges with a little water will help the seal to stay intact). Put the parcels on a non-stick baking tray. (To give them a light brown colour once cooked, you can brush each of them with beaten egg or milk.)

4   Put in the preheated oven for 15–20 minutes until golden. Leave to cool then store in a lidded container.

Variations

Mix the tuna and cheese with a little crème fraîche and cress.

Sausage lattice pie

Sent in by Julie from Coventry, who says: *'This can be eaten hot or cold, but only a small piece is required as it is very filling.'*

Makes 6–8 slices

Suitable for ages 1 year +

❄ **Will freeze before baking**

Nutrition ⬤ Fat ⬤ Saturates ◯ Sugar ◯ Salt

1 x 350g packet ready-made shortcrust pastry, or make your own (see page 165)

½ packet ready-made stuffing mix (see Tip)

450g pork sausagemeat

1 small–medium onion, peeled and finely chopped

full-fat milk or beaten egg, to glaze

NUTRITION NOTES
High in fat but ideal filling fare for children on a picnic if they are running around for hours. You can buy reduced-fat sausagemeat in some stores.

TIP
Some ready-made packet stuffing mixes are very tasty but they can be high in salt. You can make a basic stuffing of your own by mixing 100g fine fresh breadcrumbs with 2 tbsp chopped fresh mixed herbs (e.g. thyme, sage), a very little salt, black pepper and a beaten egg to bind. Other ingredients can be added as liked – e.g. chopped nuts (for children over five), seeds, chopped tomato, etc.

1 Preheat the oven to 200°C/400°F/Gas 6.

2 Cut off two-thirds of the pastry and roll thinly to line a shallow pie dish or tin (a metal dish will help the pastry to brown).

3 Prepare the stuffing mix according to pack instructions.

4 In a bowl, mix the sausagemeat with the onion and the stuffing and smooth it over the pastry in the dish.

5 Roll the remaining pastry thinly; cut into 1cm strips and lay in a lattice effect across the pie. Brush the pastry carefully with some full-fat milk or beaten egg.

6 Bake in the preheated oven for 25–30 minutes or until cooked through and the pastry is golden.

Chicken puffs

'Serve hot or cold – either is equally delicious and great for picnics,' says Jacqui from North Bedforshire, who sent the recipe to Netmums.

Makes approx. 8 puffs

Suitable for ages 1 year +

❄ **Will freeze before baking**

Nutrition ⬤ Fat ⬤ Saturates ⬭ Sugar ⬭ Salt

1 x 350g packet puff pastry

FILLING

1 medium onion, peeled and finely chopped

1 tbsp olive oil

approx. 250g cooked chicken, skinned, flesh cut into small pieces

2 tsp chopped fresh tarragon (or 1 tsp if using dried)

1 medium egg, beaten

NUTRITION NOTES
High in fat but ideal in the fresh air for hungry children. Safe picnic note: any food containing poultry should be eaten quickly or stored in an insulated container.

1   Preheat the oven to 200°C/400°F/Gas 6.

2   For the filling, sauté the onion in the oil over a medium heat until soft but not browned.

3   Put the onion in a bowl with the chicken pieces and tarragon, add the beaten egg and mix together.

4   Roll out the pastry thinly and cut into squares. Place spoonfuls of mixture on to each square, brush the edges of the pastry with cold water and fold the pastry over the filling to form a triangle. (To give them a light brown colour once cooked, you can brush each of them with beaten egg or milk.)

5   Place the puffs on a lightly greased baking sheet and bake in the preheated oven for about 15 minutes or until golden brown.

Variations

Substitute the chicken with turkey. You can also add a little (about 1 level dsp) savoury white or cheese sauce to each parcel.

Cornish pasties

350g shortcrust pastry, nice and
cold (either bought or home-made,
see page 165)

beaten egg or milk

FILLING

225g rump steak

1 medium onion, peeled

1 medium old potato, peeled

100g (about ¼) small swede,
peeled

salt and pepper

20g butter

NUTRITION NOTES
Home-made pasties will contain less
pastry and more filling than most shop-
bought pasties. The meat pasties are
high in iron and B vitamins as well as rich
in fibre and there's also some vitamin C –
for a pastry snack, a pretty healthy
package! You could use half wholemeal
flour if making your own pastry.

TIPS
If the pastry goes too brown during
cooking cover with foil.

If you have the pieces of vegetable too
big they won't cook through in time.

If you can crimp the edges while the
pasty is sitting upright (rather than lying
flat on the work surface) so that the seal
runs across the top of the pasty rather
than along the side, this will look nicer
and there is less chance that the seal will
break and the filling will spill out during
cooking. But if you make 'flat' pasties it
isn't the end of the world!

Makes 4 smallish pasties

Suitable for ages 1 year +

❋ Will freeze before baking

Nutrition ⬤ Fat ◑ Saturates ◔ Sugar ◑ Salt

1 Preheat the oven to 220°C/425°F/Gas 7.

2 Cut the steak into small pieces about 5mm square. Finely
chop the onion, potato and swede as small as you can (you
can use an electric processor if you like but don't over-
process – you still want to see the pieces).

3 Put the meat, onion, potato and swede into a bowl and
season. Combine well.

4 Divide the pastry into four balls and roll each piece out on a
lightly floured surface until they are the size of a side plate.
Use a plate to trim each to a circle. Spoon the filling equally
on to the centre of each pastry circle and top each filling
with a quarter of the butter. Brush the edges with water and
then bring together at the top to form a semi-circular pasty.
To seal you need to crimp firmly using your finger and
thumb, twisting each crimped section slightly as you go so
that the final look is a little like a rope.

5 Place the pasties on a baking tray, crimped edges
uppermost (see Tips). Using a sharp knife make a small slit
on each side of each pasty near the top. Brush each of them
with beaten egg or milk.

6 Bake in the preheated oven for 10 minutes, then turn the
heat down to 180°C/350°F/Gas 4 and cook for another
40–45 minutes, until golden brown. Serve hot or cold.

Variations

You *can* use lean steak mince or omit the meat and use
soya mince or lentils or another cooked (or canned,
drained) pulse if you like, and drizzle over a very little
vegetable stock before closing the pasties (as you won't
have the juices that run out of the steak to moisten the
filling). For cheesey ham pasties, use 225g unsmoked
gammon steak, cubed, 75g chopped mature Cheddar,
1 medium chopped leek and a finely chopped onion and
add a drizzle of vegetable or ham stock.

Biscuits and Crisps

As with pastry, active children can have biscuits and crisps sometimes – but the kind you will make at home are probably much better for their health. Getting the kids to help make them is a good way to encourage them to enjoy cooking.

Cheesey biscuits

Sent in by Czarme, who says: *'A tooth-friendly alternative to sweet biscuits!'*

Makes 10–12 biscuits

Suitable for ages 9 months +

Nutrition ⬤ Fat   ◐ Saturates   ○ Sugar   ◐ Salt

50g polyunsaturated margarine or butter

100g plain flour

50g Cheddar, freshly grated

15ml warm water

NUTRITION NOTES
Making your own simple savoury biscuits is easy and you can be sure there are no trans fats or dubious additives.

1 Preheat your oven to 190°C/375°F/Gas 5.

2 In a bowl, add the margarine to the flour and rub in to make breadcrumbs. Add the grated cheese to the bowl and stir well. Finally add the water to the mix and stir with your hands until it starts to form a dough.

3 Knead for a few minutes, then roll out on a floured surface to approximately 5mm thick. Cut out shapes with cookie cutters.

4 Place on a baking tray and brush with a little water. Bake in the preheated oven for about 10–12 minutes until golden.

5 Allow to cool completely before storing in an airtight box and they will stay really crisp for a few days (if they last that long!)

Savoury flapjacks

Great for lunchboxes and snacks.

Makes 6–8 flapjacks

Suitable for ages 1 year +

Nutrition   ● Fat   ● Saturates   ○ Sugar   ◔ Salt

1 egg

25g butter

75g Cheddar, freshly grated

70g porridge oats

NUTRITION NOTES

The oats are a good source of soluble fibre and keep hunger at bay for longer than some other grains such as wheat. The flapjacks have a medium salt rating because both butter and Cheddar cheese are high in sodium, but you could use unsalted butter if you like.

1   Preheat the oven to 180°C/350°F/Gas 4.

2   All you need to do is mix the ingredients and press into a shallow 20cm square tin. Get your children to join in if they fancy it.

3   Bake in the preheated oven for about 30–40 minutes until golden brown.

4   Once cool, cut into slices.

Vegetable crisps

Makes enough crisps for 6–8 children

Suitable for ages 1 year +

Nutrition ⬤ Fat ◐ Saturates ◐ Sugar ◐ Salt

*225g mixed root vegetables of
your choice (see Variations)*

*groundnut or sunflower oil, for
deep-frying*

a few cubes of stale bread

*sea salt and black pepper, or other
pepper of choice (see Variations)*

NUTRITION NOTES
These crisps are high in fat but
otherwise excellent – a great alternative
to commercial crisps.

1   Clean, peel or scrape the vegetables as necessary and slice into thin pieces using a vegetable peeler or a mandolin. Rinse the slices and dry them thoroughly on clean tea-towels or kitchen paper.

2   Into a large saucepan pour about 5cm deep of oil. Don't use a small pan because you don't want the oil to come higher than a third to halfway up the pan.

3   Heat the oil on the hob and add a bread cube. If it turns golden within 30 seconds or so, the oil is ready. If not, wait a minute and try again. Now add the vegetables in three batches, stirring once added. Within a short time they will turn golden. Remove them straightaway with a large slotted spoon on to kitchen paper.

4   Let the oil heat up again for a minute, adding more if necessary to make up the 5cm, then add the second batch, and so on.

5   Sprinkle the crisps with salt and pepper, allow to cool then store in an airtight container.

Variations

You can sprinkle the crisps with chilli pepper for older children. You can also cook the crisps without so much fat and without the bother of frying – just toss them in a bowl with some olive or groundnut oil and seasoning, spread out on a non-stick baking tray and bake at 200°C/400°F/Gas 6 for 15 minutes or so until golden, turning once. They need to be a very even thickness for this, though, otherwise parts will be charred while other parts won't be cooked.

You can use potatoes, sweet potatoes, parsnips, swede, carrot. You can also use beetroot but it is best to cook this separately.

Salads to Go

Here are some favourite salads that are complete meals or snacks in themselves, as they all contain carbohydrates, protein, fat and vegetables.

Bacon and egg salad

This is a bit like a cold full English breakfast!

Serves 4 children

Suitable for ages 1 year +

Nutrition   Fat   Saturates   Sugar   Salt

4 medium free-range eggs

4 slices lean unsmoked back
 bacon, cut into thin strips

150g new potatoes, cooked

1 Little Gem lettuce

8 cherry tomatoes

50g button mushrooms

2 tbsp light mayonnaise

3 tbsp low-fat bio yoghurt

a squeeze of lemon juice

freshly ground black pepper

NUTRITION NOTES

Bacon is quite high in salt so you might look for reduced-salt packs. Make sure the eggs are cooked all the way through as raw egg isn't suitable for small children.

1 Boil the eggs until hard, about 8 minutes. Meanwhile grill or dry-fry the bacon, cut the potatoes into bite-sized pieces, wash and split the lettuce into small wedges, halve the cherry tomatoes and thinly slice the mushrooms.

2 Beat together the mayo, yoghurt, lemon juice and black pepper.

3 Cool the eggs under cold running water then peel. Arrange all the salad items in containers, cut each egg into four and add to the top. Pour over the dressing.

Variations

You can use 2–3 cooked sausages, cut into small chunks, instead of the bacon. You can omit the mushrooms and use chopped spring onions instead. You can dress the salad with olive oil French dressing.

SALAD TIPS
- All these salads can be made the evening before if stored overnight in a lidded container in a cold fridge.
- If taking salad with you on a picnic or away on any warm day make sure that you pack it in an insulated container to avoid any chance of food poisoning. You can buy insulated containers of all sizes and insulated lunch boxes.
- For any salads that are not going to be eaten for several hours it is best to avoid those made with fresh meat (e.g. chicken).
- Also take care with cooked pasta and rice salads as levels of bacteria in cooked grains can build up more quickly than in leaf type salads.
- Pack individual salads in sturdy containers with lids that are very secure to avoid spillage. Don't forget plastic spoon/fork as necessary – the salads in these pages won't need a knife.

Pasta salad

This salad is also nice served freshly made and warm at home.

Serves 4 children

Suitable for ages 1 year +

Nutrition   ⬭ Fat   ⬭ Saturates   ⬭ Sugar   ⬭ Salt

200g (dry weight) pasta shapes of choice (see Tip)

2 skinless chicken breast fillets, cut into bite-sized slices

1 tbsp olive oil

2 medium tomatoes, roughly chopped

1 yellow pepper, seeded and roughly chopped

1 small red onion, peeled and roughly chopped

2 tbsp olive oil French dressing (see page 100)

chopped parsley to garnish (optional)

NUTRITION NOTES

This is a lovely healthy salad which tastes great and is rich in fibre, vitamins and minerals.

TIP

Spirals or pasta bows work well in this salad. Choose a very good quality pasta so that it doesn't break up or go soggy.

1   Cook the pasta according to packet instructions, drain and put into a bowl.

2   Meanwhile, heat half the oil in a large non-stick frying pan and sauté the chicken slices over a medium-high heat until cooked through, about 5 minutes. Remove with a slotted spoon and add to the pasta.

3   Add the tomato, pepper and onion to the frying pan with the remainder of the oil. Sauté over a medium-high heat for about 20 minutes or until turning golden and tender.

4   Now take the pan off the heat and stir the French dressing into the vegetables. Tip the vegetables and all their juices from the pan into the pasta and chicken. Stir well to combine and garnish with parsley, if using.

Variations

You can add extra French dressing to the salad if you like. You can omit the chicken and simply add small cubes of feta, halloumi or firm mozzarella to the pan towards the end of the vegetable cooking time. You can use wholewheat pasta. For older children you can drizzle some chilli sauce into the salad.

You can make a similar salad to the pasta one by roasting Mediterranean vegetables and tipping them into the pasta. You can cook larger pieces of chicken in with the vegetables in that case.

Pizza salad

Serves 4–6 children

Suitable for ages 1 year +

Nutrition   ◯ Fat   ◯ Saturates   ◯ Sugar   ◯ Salt

*200g pasta shapes, e.g. penne or
spirals*

2 tbsp ready-made mayonnaise

*2 tbsp ready-made pizza tomato
sauce*

100g lean ham, cut into strips

*100g cooked chicken (no skin or
bone)*

50g sliced pepperoni

8 cherry tomatoes, halved

3 tbsp cooked sweetcorn kernels

50g Cheddar, finely grated

a handful of basil leaves (optional)

NUTRITION NOTES

This salad contains a wide range of
nutrients, including a variety of
vitamins and minerals. Try wholewheat
pasta for a change: it has a good texture
for eating cold, and contains more fibre
and B vitamins, magnesium and iron.

1   Cook the pasta in a large pan of boiling water (with a little
salt if liked) with a dash of cooking oil added to prevent
sticking, for the amount of time stated on the packet,
usually about 10 minutes. Drain and tip into a serving bowl.

2   Mix together the mayo and pizza sauce and combine with
the pasta. Clean the visible inside edges of the bowl with
kitchen paper.

3   Now top the pasta with the rest of the ingredients,
spreading them evenly around as you would top a real
pizza, and finishing with the cheese and basil leaves.

Variations

Alter the 'topping' according to what you have: you could
omit the pepperoni and add extra chicken; you could swap
the corn for finely diced yellow pepper.

Desserts and drinks

Every child enjoys sweet tastes. But we're constantly told that sugar is bad for our children, so is dessert yet another thing to feel guilty about? In this chapter we have brought together some sweet treats and drinks that can be enjoyed without too much worry as, while most of them do contain sugar, they also contain a range of other nutritional goodies, such as protein, fibre, vitamins or minerals. They are also brilliantly devoid of artificial additives, preservatives, thickeners, etc., of the kind that you will find in almost every dessert in the supermarket.

Making these desserts really isn't hard, so even if you think you can't do it, give them a try — and enjoy them.

Cold Desserts

Dessert time is the ideal occasion – along with breakfast and between-meal snacks – to get plenty of fruit into your child's diet. Try these quick dessert ideas.

Rhubarb fool

Sent in by Stacey from Bromley, who says: *'Very simple and you can substitute the rhubarb for any other fruit – strawberries, raspberries, exotic fruit. I use plastic cups for the kids instead of serving glasses.'*

Serves 4 children

Suitable for ages 1 year +

Nutrition   ◼ Fat   ◼ Saturates   ◼ Sugar   ◼ Salt

250g rhubarb, trimmed and
  coarsely chopped

55g caster sugar

a little water, about 100ml

$1/2$ tsp ground cinnamon (optional)

180ml whipping cream

1 tbsp icing sugar

250ml prepared vanilla custard

NUTRITION NOTES
Rhubarb is great for children who have trouble with constipation. Cinnamon is a natural sweetener that means you can use less sugar with sour fruits.

1   Combine the rhubarb in a saucepan with the caster sugar, water and cinnamon. Bring to the boil, reduce the heat and simmer, uncovered, for 10 minutes or until the fruit is tender. Transfer to a bowl, cover and refrigerate for an hour.

2   Beat the cream and icing sugar together in a small bowl until peaks form. Stir the custard into the rhubarb, then fold the whipped cream mixture into the rhubarb mixture.

3   Divide the fool among four 160ml serving glasses. Refrigerate, covered, for an hour before serving.

Variations
Fruit fools are such a quick and easy dessert: try making them using gooseberries, stewed apples or poached raspberries.

Fresh fruit salad

Sent in by Diana from Birmingham, who says: 'My children aged four and six love making fruit salad. We go shopping for the ingredients and I let them choose what fruits to buy (depending on what's ripe, and in season).

'When we start making the fruit salad, I get them to use their senses to look at, taste, smell and touch the fruits. We look at the labels to see what country the fruits are from. They then help to cut up the softer fruits (I peel and core them, as necessary) and put them in a big bowl. They then spoon their own portion into a bowl.

'It's amazing what they will eat, when they've made it themselves...

'A few ideas include: strawberries, apple, banana, peach, pineapple, tangerine segments, mango, melon, kiwi, pear, cherries etc., etc. Sprinkle with a bit of sugar and cover for a few hours in the fridge and some of the natural juices will come out of the fruits to make it good!!

'Add bananas just before serving, and to keep fruits from browning either dip into some lemon water or sprinkle lemon juice over the whole bunch and toss together.

'A blob of vanilla ice-cream on top of the fruit salad seems to help entice more reluctant fruit eaters!'

NUTRITION NOTES

Fresh fruit salad is a perfect dessert for children and is infinitely variable. Most versions contain lots of vitamin C, fibre and potassium. For children who like their fruit salads a bit more 'runny' you can pour fresh orange juice (or apple juice or indeed any other juice which matches the ingredients) over the salad in the bowl and stir well.

TIP

When keeping fruit salad, store, covered, in the fridge. While bananas may discolour, most fruit salad keeps quite well for a day or two, although it will begin to lose vitamin C.

Quick cheesecake

Sent in by Jane from Pinner.

Serves 4–6 children

Suitable for ages 1 year +

Nutrition ● Fat ● Saturates ◌ Sugar ◌ Salt

BASE

150g digestive biscuits

75g butter

TOPPING

1 x 250g tub mascarpone cheese

25g caster sugar

1 tsp vanilla extract (optional)

juice of ½ lemon (optional)

1 Put the biscuits in a bag and crush them with a rolling pin until they are crumbs (choose your moment as it can be fantastic therapy!)

2 Gently melt the butter in a saucepan then add the biscuit crumbs. Mix well then press into the base of a loose-bottomed 17cm cake tin. If you don't have a loose-bottomed cake tin then use any round dish lined with greaseproof paper. Use a potato masher for a really compact job. Put in the fridge for 30 minutes.

3 Mix the cheese, sugar, vanilla and lemon (if using) together, pour over the top of the biscuit base, smooth over and chill.

Variations

- Use crème fraîche, cream cheese or ricotta cheese instead of mascarpone cheese.

- Add in any over-ripe fruit you have – bruised bananas or slightly old strawberries. Use a food processor to whiz them up together with the cheese and sugar topping to vary this dessert.

- Use ginger biscuits instead of digestives.

- To make the topping more firm you can use gelatine or egg white, but who has the time for that and it tastes just as good without.

Summer pudding

Sent in by Bev from South Devon, who says: *'This is based on my mum's recipe – it was such a treat when she used to serve it up in the late summer.'*

Serves 4–6 children

Suitable for ages 9 months +

Nutrition   ◯ Fat   ◯ Saturates   ● Sugar   ◯ Salt

8 slices white bread, approx. (See Tip)

100g caster sugar

5 tbsp water

750g mixed soft summer fruit like blackberries, strawberries, raspberries, blueberries and redcurrants

NUTRITION NOTES
Possibly one of the healthiest cold puds you can make – really high in vitamin C, fibre and plant chemicals and bread is so much lower in fat than pastry!

SERVING SUGGESTION
Cream, crème fraîche or natural or Greek yoghurt.

TIP
It's good if the bread is a bit stale. Ready-sliced bread doesn't go stale very easily because of the preservatives in it, so it is best to stick to a whole loaf.

1 Cut the crusts off the bread and discard. Reserve half the slices, and use the remaining slices to line a medium pudding basin.

2 Put the sugar and water in a large pan and heat gently, stirring until all the sugar is dissolved. Add the fruit and simmer for 10 minutes.

3 Add half the hot fruit mixture to the bread-lined bowl, then cover with a layer of bread. Add the remaining fruit and cover with the remaining bread.

4 Cover the basin with a saucer which sits on the bread and add a food tin to act as a weight. Chill for 12 hours.

5 To serve, remove the tin and the saucer. Place a serving dish over the top of the basin and invert, shaking gently so the pudding comes out.

Variations
For a very quick summer pudding you can just spoon the stewed fruit mixture into individual bowls and add 2–3 small pieces of bread to each, pushing down well. Leave until the bread has soaked up the juice.

Chocolate dip with fresh fruit

This is a good party dish.

Serves 4 children

Suitable for ages 1 year +

Nutrition   ◯ Fat   ◯ Saturates   ◯ Sugar   ◯ Salt

150g block good-quality milk or
  plain chocolate

1 tbsp sunflower or groundnut oil

a selection of fresh fruits, peeled
  and cut into bite-sized chunks if
  necessary (e.g. pineapple,
  strawberries, melon, seedless
  satsuma segments, mango,
  grapes)

some bite-sized marshmallows

NUTRITION NOTES
This is a great way to get fruit-phobic
children to learn to love it.

TIP
Chocolate can be melted in a dish on a
low heat in the microwave as well.

1   Break the chocolate into small pieces in a heatproof bowl
    that will sit over a saucepan. Add a little water to the pan
    then add the bowl of chocolate and bring to low simmer,
    making sure that the bowl doesn't touch the water. Leave
    until the chocolate is melted.

2   Add the oil to the melted chocolate and stir gently. This will
    help the chocolate sauce stay runny for longer when it
    cools down.

3   Arrange the fruits and marshmallows on a large platter and
    put the melted chocolate sauce in a bowl in the centre. For
    older children you can put the pieces of fruit on to wooden
    cocktail sticks. Let the children help themselves — with
    plenty of kitchen paper or napkins to hand.

Variations
You could of course dish each child his or her portion on an
individual plate with a little bowl of the sauce. White
chocolate can be used but darker chocolate contrasts better
with the sweetness of the fruit.

Instant Black Forest trifle

This trifle (and the many variations) is even easier than a trifle made with bought custard – you don't even have to make jelly – and it is gorgeous.

Serves 4 children

Suitable for ages 1 year +

Nutrition ● Fat ● Saturates ● Sugar ○ Salt

2 large chocolate muffins

200g stoned fresh or canned black or red cherries

cherry or other red juice (if using canned cherries use the can juice)

4 tbsp red fruit coulis (see next page)

1 x 250ml tub mascarpone cheese

200ml double cream, whipped

TIP

For a lighter trifle you can mix the mascarpone half and half with Greek yoghurt, and for an even lighter version you can use 8% fat fromage frais beaten with a little icing sugar. You can also beat the mascarpone with some skimmed milk to lighten it.

If you are using canned cherries, choose something else to decorate the top – e.g. glacé cherries or fresh small strawberries – as the cherry juice will bleed on to the cream, or drain them very thoroughly and dry on kitchen paper.

1 Break the muffins up into pieces and arrange in the base of a trifle bowl with three-quarters of the cherries.

2 Drizzle in the cherry juice and then the fruit coulis.

3 Spoon in the mascarpone and smooth over.

4 Cover this with the whipped cream and decorate with the remaining cherries, well drained (see Tip).

Variations

Use plain sponge cake or Madeira cake instead of the muffins. Use raspberries, strawberries, bananas, orange pieces or whatever softish fruit you like. You can use thick custard instead of the mascarpone.

Fruit coulis

It is easy to make your own fruit coulis, and as the small bottles of coulis on sale are really expensive, it might be a good idea!

SERVING SUGGESTION
Use with ice-cream, chocolate cake, Madeira cake and chocolate mousse. Makes a great change from creamy toppings.

If you have any soft fruit such as strawberries, raspberries or blackberries, just put them in a pan with 2 tbsp water, 1 dsp lemon juice and 1 tbsp icing sugar for each 150g fruit. Simmer until just softened, then blend in the blender and pour through a large sieve (to remove any pips) into a bowl with a pouring lip. If you don't have a blender you can simply mash the fruit through the sieve. Pour into tightly lidded plastic containers and freeze, or store in the fridge (it will keep for several days).

Ice-creams

Why buy ice-cream when you can make your own as easily as this? Go for the best-quality ingredients that you can, and taste the difference!

'Saints' creamy banana ice-cream

Sent in by Vicky, from Stoke on Trent, who says: '*You won't believe* that this is just *mashed banana, it's so creamy.* I make it for my daughter as I don't give her sweets and ice-cream because I worry about her teeth. This way I can give her a treat, which she loves, and also give her *some hidden goodness!* It's also *good for us mums and dads who are trying to lose weight.* Brilliant!'

Serves about 4 children

Suitable for ages 6 months +

Nutrition   ◯ Fat   ◯ Saturates   ◯ Sugar   ◯ Salt

6 nicely ripened bananas (the skins should have some brown speckling)

NUTRITION NOTES
Bananas are high in potassium and fibre.

SERVING SUGGESTION
Would go well with some sliced strawberries.

1   Peel and wrap each banana individually in clingfilm. Place in the freezer for an hour or so.

2   Take out of the freezer and mash. This can be quite difficult: cut them up into manageable pieces and then mash with a potato masher or blender.

3   Put in a bowl, cover with clingfilm and place again in the freezer for another hour.

4   Pull out of the freezer and mash again, this time with a fork, and serve.

Lemon ice-cream

Sent in by Davina from Sheffield.

Serves 4–6 children

Suitable for ages 5 years + (contains raw eggs, not suitable for pre school-age children)

Nutrition ⬤ Fat ⬤ Saturates ⬤ Sugar ◯ Salt

3 medium eggs, separated

280ml double cream

110g caster sugar

3 tbsp lemon juice

NUTRITION NOTES

Home-made ice-cream is high in fat but unlike many commercial ices, will contain no trans fats.

1 In a mixing bowl, beat the egg yolks until frothy and light.

2 Whisk the egg whites in another bowl until stiff, add half the sugar and whisk until stiff again.

3 Beat the cream in a large mixing bowl until it forms soft peaks then fold in the egg yolks, whites, the rest of the sugar and the lemon juice. Turn into a suitable container and freeze.

4 Remove from the freezer about 20 minutes before serving.

Chocolate ice-cream

Sent in by Milly's granny.

Serves 4–6 children

Suitable for ages 5 years + (contains raw eggs, not suitable for pre school-age children)

Nutrition ● Fat ● Saturates ◐ Sugar ◯ Salt

2 heaped tbsp caster sugar

4 tbsp water

175g dark chocolate. (Use a plain chocolate with a high cocoa solid content – about 60–70%.)

3 medium egg yolks

250ml whipping cream

NUTRITION NOTES
The chocolate and egg yolks contain iron and a range of other vitamins and minerals.

1   Put the sugar and water in a microwaveable bowl and heat in the microwave for a minute on high. Stir in the sugar until dissolved then replace in the microwave for a further minute.

2   Break the chocolate into the blender, add the hot syrup and blend until smooth then add the egg yolks and blend again.

3   Gently fold the whipped cream into the chocolate mixture. Pour into a suitable freezable container and freeze.

4   Remove from the freezer about 20 minutes before serving.

Variations
For adults you can add 1–2 tbsp brandy at step 3.

Hot Desserts

While there is little time these days to make traditional hot puddings from scratch, there are several quicker – and healthier – alternatives here for you to try, all of which will be much appreciated by the family.

Baked apples

Sent in by Noreen from Havering.

Serves 4 children

Suitable for ages 9 months +

Nutrition ◯ Fat   ◯ Saturates   ◯ Sugar   ◯ Salt

4 cooking apples (Bramleys are best)

8 tsp (approx.) soft brown sugar

4 tbsp (approx.) dried mixed fruit or sultanas

4 small knobs unsalted butter

1 tsp ground cinnamon

NUTRITION NOTES
Apples are a fantastic source of soluble fibre and potassium, and are linked with a reduction in asthma symptoms in children. Dried fruit is rich in iron.

SERVING SUGGESTION
Serve with ice-cream or custard or enjoy simply as they are.

1 Preheat the oven to 180°C/350°F/Gas 4.

2 Scoop out the core from the top of each apple, leaving a well. Don't cut quite all the way through to the bottom but get all the pips out. Score the skin horizontally around the centre of the apple, to stop the skin bursting as it cooks.

3 Stuff each apple with a couple of tsp of brown sugar and some dried fruit to fill. Place in a shallow baking dish, and top each apple centre with a knob of butter. Put a couple of tbsp water in the bottom of the dish and sprinkle the apples with cinnamon.

4 Bake in the preheated oven for 45 minutes or until the sugar begins to caramelise and the apples are tender. Check once or twice during cooking to make sure that the dish isn't drying out – add a little extra water if it is needed as you want some caramelised juices in the bottom to spoon over the apples when serving.

Variations

You can use mincemeat as a stuffing and for children over five you can add chopped nuts. You can use apple juice to add to the dish instead of water. And you can drizzle a little golden syrup over the apples before baking them.

Quick banana pud idea

Sent in by Sam from Kent: 'Just take a couple of bananas and cut them into chunks. Fry in a little butter with juice from ½ orange (or just use orange juice!) and a sprinkling of brown sugar. When hot and beginning to caramelise, put in bowls and serve with Greek yoghurt, or custard or ice-cream for a special treat.

'You can add chunks of pineapple for a change.

'You could also use the pudding as a filling for pancakes' (below).

Sweet pancakes

Sent in by Gabrielle from Guildford.

Makes 8 smallish pancakes

Suitable for ages 9 months +

Nutrition   Fat   Saturates   Sugar   Salt

110g plain flour

a pinch of salt

1 medium egg, beaten

275ml semi-skimmed milk

a little groundnut or sunflower oil

TO SERVE

1 lemon

4 tsp caster sugar

TIP

You can keep the pancakes warm in the oven, if you like, covered with foil.

1. Sieve the flour and salt into a mixing bowl. Make a well in the middle of the flour, pour in the egg and gradually beat in with a fork or whisk.

2. Pour in the milk in stages, making sure that the batter is well mixed before adding the next splash.

3. Heat a small to medium non-stick frying pan or griddle on the hob until hot with a tsp of oil. Pour in just enough batter to coat the pan, let it cook for a few minutes or until the underside is speckled golden brown, then flip over and cook for another 30 seconds. Remove to a warm plate. Continue cooking the remaining pancakes, adding a tsp of oil each time and letting it heat up until very hot before adding the next lot of batter.

4. Serve with lemon wedges and a sprinkling of caster sugar or with the apple filling opposite or the banana filling (above).

Apple and cinnamon pancake filling

Serves 4 children

Suitable for ages 9 months +

Nutrition   ◯ Fat   ◯ Saturates   ● Sugar   ◯ Salt

1 or 2 dessert apples, peeled and grated

2 tbsp sultanas

1/2 tsp ground cinnamon

1 tbsp brown caster sugar

SERVING SUGGESTION
If you prefer you can pour over a tbsp of apple juice or water and heat the filling through in the microwave on medium high for a minute or two. Stir before serving.

1   Mix the grated apple, sultanas, cinnamon and sugar to taste.

2   Place in the pancakes and fold over. If the pancakes are hot from the pan they will gently warm the filling.

Crumbles

If you've no time to make a pie for dessert, you've certainly time to make a crumble! Crumbles have to be the most forgiving of all hot puddings and, even better, they are delicious cold too. Choose your filling wisely and they can be reasonably healthy for the kids as well.

Basic apple crumble

125g plain flour

25g demerara sugar

75g butter, cold

3 medium or 2 large cooking
   apples (e.g. Bramleys)

25g (approx.) caster sugar (or
   demerara)

Serves 4 children

Suitable for ages 9 months +

❋ **Will freeze** (best frozen before cooking)

Nutrition 🔵 Fat 🔵 Saturates ⚫ Sugar 🔵 Salt

NUTRITION NOTES

While a crumble topping is quite high in fat and sugar, if your children aren't keen on fresh fruit a crumble is a great way to get fruit vitamins, fibre, minerals and plant chemicals into them without a fuss – virtually *all* kids love crumble! You can cut down on sugar by using cinnamon or you could try fructose (fruit sugar) now and then; you use less fructose than sugar because it is sweeter (however, large amounts can cause problems so use sensibly).

SERVING SUGGESTION

Crème fraîche, custard or vanilla ice-cream.

1   Preheat the oven to 180°C/350°F/Gas 4.

2   In a large mixing bowl, combine the flour and demerara sugar thoroughly. Cut the butter into small pieces and add to the bowl, then, using cold, dry fingers, rub the butter into the flour until it resembles fine breadcrumbs. Set aside.

3   Peel and core the apples and slice them into the base of a medium ovenproof dish. Sprinkle over the caster sugar and 1–2 tbsp water. For early season apples you may need a little more sugar. Stir to combine and flatten them down evenly.

4   Spread the crumble mix evenly over the top to cover all the apples and bake in the preheated oven for about 30 minutes or until the top is golden and the apples are bubbling. Allow to cool a little before serving.

Crumble variations

Toppings

- Add 2 tbsp porridge oats (not the instant kind) to the dry mix.

- Add 2 tbsp chopped mixed nuts at the end of mixing (after the butter) — only for children over five years old. These give a lovely crunchy texture.

- You can use muesli instead of the oats but remember not to overcook the topping or any dried fruit it contains may burn.

- For people who don't feel confident about mixing the cold butter into the flour you can warm the butter in a small pan or in the microwave until melted and pour it slowly over the dry mix, stirring, until it is combined. This produces a different texture from the 'breadcrumbs' method but is delicious.

- One last topping variation for children over five is to combine 2 tbsp chopped nuts, 1 tbsp sunflower seeds and 75g porridge oats in a bowl. Melt 1 tbsp golden syrup in a pan with 25g butter and 1 tbsp brown sugar. Stir the melted mix into the oat mix and combine well.

Fruit

- You can add a little ground cinnamon or a cinnamon stick to the apple mix.

- Use peeled, cored, sliced pears (you may need less sugar), or chunks of rhubarb (you may need more sugar), or stoned and quartered plums.

- Combine the apples with either blackcurrants, raspberries, blackberries, blueberries or sultanas. If using sultanas they are even better if you soak them in a little water for 30 minutes before using. Use about one-fifth or a quarter of the small fruits to the apples.

- Use half apples and half pears.

- In late autumn and winter you can make a lovely dried fruit and banana crumble using apricots, prunes, apple rings or any combination of dried fruit that you like to try. For apricot and banana crumble simply simmer 200g dried apricots until plumped and tender, chop and add to the baking dish with the cooking juices and 2 medium sliced bananas and the juice of $\frac{1}{2}$ lemon, mixing well. There is no need for added sugar. Add whatever topping you like.

Pies and tarts

Home-made pies have several advantages over most commercial ones: they contain a much higher ratio of fruit to pastry; if you make your own pastry you are avoiding trans fats (see page 25); and you can use a little less sugar (some of the supermarket pies are so very sweet). There is no need to make a fruit pie with a double crust (top *and* bottom): it saves time and fat if you just put a lid on a fruit base. We start with a very basic apple pie recipe, which you can jazz up or vary according to how you feel and what you have.

Apple pie

700g Bramley apples

75g soft brown sugar

1 tsp ground cinnamon

1 tbsp plain flour

25g butter, diced

250g shortcrust pastry (see page 165)

2 tsp white caster sugar

NUTRITION NOTES
Both the fruit pies here are high in fat, sugar and calories, so a small portion is called for if the family eat fruit pies very regularly.

TIP
You can put a pie funnel in the centre of the dish to help keep the pastry from getting moist.

SERVING SUGGESTION
Serve with cream, custard, ice-cream.

Serves 6 children or a family of 4

Suitable for ages 9 months +

❄ **Will freeze before baking**

Nutrition ● Fat ● Saturates ● Sugar ◯ Salt

1   Preheat the oven to 190°C/375°F/Gas 5.

2   Peel, core and slice the apples thinly and put a layer of the apple slices in the base of a 900ml pie dish.

3   Mix the brown sugar, cinnamon and flour together in a bowl. Sprinkle the apples with some of the flour mix and repeat the layers until the dish is filled, then dot with the butter.

4   Roll out the pastry until just larger than the pie dish. Brush the edges of the dish with water, then cover the apples with the pastry, firming down the edges. Use any leftover pastry to decorate the top.

5   Brush the pastry with water and sprinkle with caster sugar, then bake in the preheated oven for 40–45 minutes or until the top is golden and the apples are cooked through.

Variations
Any of the fruit mixes described for crumbles would be nice.

Upside-down fruit pie

This pie is a simple version of *tarte tatin* – even more delicious than apple pie and just as easy to make. You will need a medium heavy-based ovenproof frying pan though, and a rolling pin.

Serves 4–6

Suitable for ages 1 year +

Nutrition   ● Fat   ● Saturates   ● Sugar   ○ Salt

*6–8 crisp eating apples, such as
Cox's, peeled, cored and
quartered*

75g caster sugar

*50g unsalted butter, cut into small
pieces*

1 x 375g packet puff pastry

NUTRITION NOTES
Yes this is quite naughty nutrition-wise as it is high in fat and sugar but contains more 'goodies' (e.g. fibre, vitamin C) than most of the desserts you can buy from the frozen counter or local bakery. A superb occasional treat for active kids!

SERVING SUGGESTION
Nice with thick cream or crème fraîche.

*TIP
To turn out, cover the pan with the
serving plate and invert and flip the tart
on to it.*

1   Preheat the oven to 180°C/350°F/Gas 4.

2   Heat the sugar and half the butter in a medium ovenproof frying pan over a medium-low heat on the hob, watching it all the time, until it has caramelised (turned a rich brown). Remove from the heat immediately this happens.

3   Now arrange the apple quarters in one layer in the pan so that they are tightly packed. If there are any gaps you need to fill them in with more apple. Dot with the remaining butter and cook gently for a few minutes on the hob then leave to cool slightly.

4   Meanwhile, roll out the pastry to a circle just bigger than the frying pan. Drape it over a rolling pin and cover the apples. Tuck the pastry down the sides of the pan (inside).

5   Bake in the preheated oven for 25 minutes then remove from the oven. Leave to cool for 10 minutes then turn out on to a serving plate so that the pastry is underneath and you have a lovely caramelised topping of apples with a little thick juice.

Variations
Make the tart with chunks of pineapple or with pear quarters.

Drinks

While children need no drink other than water and milk, it is nice to have a few alternatives to commercial fizzy drinks and squashes up your sleeve. The drinks here are all easy to make and nutritious too.

Hot chocolate

Great for a nutritious drink, especially in the winter.

NUTRITION NOTES
Hot chocolate is a great evening drink for kids as it will help them to get a good night's sleep. The calcium it contains is sometimes called 'nature's tranquilliser' and milk also contains tryptophan – a protein which converts into serotonin, a good-mood-producing brain chemical.

Put a few lumps of good-quality dark cooking chocolate (3 or 4 lumps per child) and melt gently in a saucepan. Once melted add milk (approx. 250ml per child) and stir until mixed.

Pour out into mugs and top with a blob of whipped cream. Decorate if you're feeling frivolous with mini marshmallows or chocolate powder.

Variations
You can also get yummy instant hot chocolate granules that don't include too much sugar. You just mix with hot milk so you don't have to go through the chocolate melting process.

'It's always *good to add variety* into your diet so change your hot chocolate slightly by using *soya* milk or *goat's milk* – my children don't seem to notice the slight difference in taste when it's *masked by the chocolate,'* says Netmums member Sasha.

Smoothies

Smoothies are great: they're refreshing, children love them and they're an easy way to get everyone eating more fruit. They include the whole fruit so the vitamins and other nutrients are in a very natural form, combined with the fruit's fibre, and this means that there are fewer fluctuations in blood sugar levels. The other bonus is that children tend to like smoothies made of fruits that they would otherwise not touch. So, by drinking them, they get used to a larger variety of real fruit tastes.

- Peel, core and chop the fruit as necessary into even pieces. Avoid hard fruits which won't blend well: a soft ripe dessert pear would be fine, for instance, but a Conference pear wouldn't. You can use apples but they need to be finely chopped and won't become as smooth as some other fruits.

- You don't have to have a special smoothie maker: a liquidiser or hand-held blender works just as well. Simply throw any fruit you have in the kitchen into the container and liquidise.

- You can jazz up your smoothies by adding different milks and yoghurts. It's a great way to introduce other forms of milk, such as soya milk, just to add a little variety into their diet. Or you can make a pure fruit smoothie just with fruit and water or water/fruit juice.

- As a general rule you would use one portion of fruit (e.g. a banana or a small banana and a handful of strawberries) to 100ml liquid. But the liquid content of fruits varies, so start with a little less liquid than you might think as you can easily add more.

Continued

- Start by blending the fruit with just a little liquid first, then add more liquid as needed and blend again.

- For a fuller flavour add 1–2 tbsp fruit coulis to the smoothie – choose one that goes with the fruit you are using (see page 186). With bland fruits you can add a dash of lemon juice to lift.

- For the best taste, make sure the smoothie is served really cold.

- A made-up smoothie will keep in the fridge for the day but you may need to re-blend before serving or give it a good stir.

- All the smoothies mentioned here are suitable for children over a year old. The smoothies should be made with whole milk for children aged one to two. Semi-skimmed milk can be given to children from two to five, and skimmed milk can be given over five.

'The *best smoothie we've made* included healthy doses of *strawberries, bananas*, a few *chocolate chips* and *soya milk*. MMMmmmmm... Perfect for those on a *dairy-free* diet and oh, so healthy.'
Vicky from Bristol

Here are some ideas sent in by Netmums members:

FRUITS

bananas

strawberries

raspberries, blueberries (the frozen variety make the drink nice and refreshing)

oranges

passionfruit

kiwi fruit

mango

LIQUIDS

cow's milk

goat's milk

sheep's milk

soya milk

oat milk

buffalo milk

water

Greek yoghurt

natural yoghurt

fruit juice

'Smoothies are the best thing ever. My little one loves them and I serve them to get her used to fruit she has not had before or does not like. Fortunately she was an early straw drinker (10 months) so for me smoothies are just the best and healthiest convenience fast food around for kids. I normally use whatever fruit I have around. In summer you can freeze half the fruit and add ice cubes to make a frozen smoothie, a much healthier version of the commercial milkshakes you get.' Ineke from Hants

And here are some more ideas – all for two portions:

GREEN SMOOTHIE

2 kiwi fruits

3 rings pineapple

200ml apple juice

MANGO AND PEACH

1 ripe mango

1 ripe peach

100ml orange juice

100ml coconut milk or other milk

PEAR AND RASPBERRY

1 ripe dessert pear

100g raspberries

250ml natural bio yoghurt

a little runny honey

added milk as necessary.

'Really basic smoothie I make in the mornings, which my son loves: 1 banana, 2 oranges, Greek honey yoghurt and 1 passionfruit. Blend and sieve, delicious!!!' Carolina from Bristol

Bakes, biscuits and cakes

Long ago, a shop-bought cake was a treat or something only rich people had. Now, a home-made cake is a rare and special thing that we seldom make time for. And yet there is something so special, homely and, well, motherly about home-made cakes — and the smell of baking will linger in your children's memories long after the cakes have been eaten. By just having the basic ingredients in the cupboard we can all rustle up a simple batch of biscuits or muffins or a teatime cake for our family and visiting mums and kids. It's very rewarding and, of course, kids love to help.

In this chapter we have got together a selection of easy baking recipes which are generally more healthy than their supermarket counterparts. They don't contain that long list of additives, and cakes or biscuits made yourself with butter are better than those made with hardened (hydrogenated/trans) fats, which is what you get with many commercial products.

Large Cakes and Loaves

'When our *family needs cheering up* – *on a wet weekend or a stressful Monday, or just when we're a bit out of sorts – I make a cake. Likewise, if a friend or other mum is going through a tough time, I will often make them a cake too. It isn't going to change the world, but it's my way of doing something positive and sharing it and showing I care. And the secret? Baking cakes is easy – why does everyone seem so surprised by it!'* Julia, mum to Finn, Rory and Aidan

Apple cake

Sent in by Rachel from Newcastle.

Makes 10–12 slices

Suitable for ages 1 year +

Nutrition   ⬭ Fat   ⬭ Saturates   ⬤ Sugar   ⬭ Salt

225g self-raising flour

a pinch of salt

1 tsp ground cinnamon

a pinch of freshly grated nutmeg

115g butter, roughly chopped

350g cooking apples

115g soft brown sugar

2–3 tbsp milk

1–2 tbsp demerara sugar

NUTRITION NOTES
Apples are high in plant chemicals which may help improve lung function in children prone to asthma.

1   Preheat the oven to 180°C/350°F/Gas 4. Lightly grease a 23cm round cake tin and sit it on a baking sheet.

2   Sift the flour, salt and spices into a bowl and rub in the butter until the mixture resembles fine breadcrumbs.

3   Peel, core and finely chop the apples and mix them with the soft brown sugar. Stir into the flour mixture and beat in enough milk to form a soft batter. Spoon the mixture into the prepared tin and spread it evenly. Sprinkle with the demerara sugar to give the cake a crunchy topping.

4   Place the baking sheet in the preheated oven and bake the cake for 40–45 minutes or until firm to the touch. Allow to cool.

Variations
You could add 100g sultanas (pre-soaked in a little water for 20 minutes) at step 3, or use ripe dessert pears instead of half the apples.

Fruit cake

Sent in by Elizabeth from Reading.

Makes 12–14 slices

Suitable for ages 1 year +

Nutrition   ⬭ Fat   ⬭ Saturates   ⬤ Sugar   ⬭ Salt

250ml or 1 American cup strong
 tea

450g dried mixed fruit

175g soft brown sugar

1 tsp mixed spice

1 medium egg, beaten

250g plain flour

$^1/_2$ tsp bicarbonate of soda

NUTRITION NOTES

This is a great nutritious cake and
contains no added fat. All that dried fruit
means it is rich in iron and fibre.

1   In a bowl, mix together the tea, dried fruit, soft brown sugar
and spice. Leave for an hour at least so the fruit soaks up
the tea and spices.

2   Preheat the oven to 180ºC/350ºF/Gas 4. Grease and line a
1kg cake tin.

3   Mix the beaten egg into the fruit mixture, then sieve in the
flour and bicarbonate of soda.

4   Spoon the mixture into the prepared tin and bake in the
preheated oven for 1$^1/_2$ hours. Allow to cool.

Five-cup fruit loaf

Sent in by Nina from Glasgow, who says: *'Everyone loves this one. It is absolutely foolproof and makes a nice sticky loaf out of nearly anything in the store cupboard, and has virtually no fat at all.*

'To measure the ingredients you just use a cup or mug. An ordinary coffee mug will make enough for a big 1kg loaf tin, a small cup enough for a 500g one. Use the same mug/cup for all the ingredients though.'

Makes 1 or 2 loaves

Suitable for ages 1 year + but if you use muesli it will contain nuts and should not be given to children under 5

Nutrition ⬒ Fat * ◯ Saturates ● Sugar ⬒ Salt * (* depending on cereal and milk used)

1 cup sugar

1 cup chopped dates or alternative (see Variations)

1 cup any kind of robust breakfast cereal (oats, bran flakes, muesli, etc.)

1 cup milk

1 cup self-raising flour

NUTRITION NOTES

Another low-fat high-fibre recipe which shows that cake can be good for you! Using carrot or banana will reduce the total sugar content of the loaf but even if you use carrots the sugar is still RED.

1. Preheat the oven to 180°C/350°F/Gas 4. Line the loaf tin with greaseproof paper.

2. In a bowl, mix together the first four ingredients and leave to soak for an hour or so.

3. Add the self-raising flour and mix well. The mix will be very runny compared to most cake mixes.

4. Pour into the tin and bake in the preheated oven for an hour or so until the cake is firm and a knife comes out clean.

5. Allow to cool and keep in an airtight tin. The longer you keep it the better. Eat sliced with butter.

Variations

You can use whatever fruit you have – mixed fruit, chopped apricots, mashed bananas – or you can use grated carrot.

Banana, pecan and fudge loaf

Sent in by Donna from Aberdeen.

Makes about 20 slices

Suitable for ages 5 years +

Nutrition   ⬤ Fat   ⬤ Saturates   ⬤ Sugar   ⬤ Salt

2 ripe bananas, mashed

2 medium eggs, beaten

110g butter, melted

1 x 125g tub toffee yoghurt

110g light muscovado sugar

225g self-raising flour

$^{1}/_{2}$ tsp baking powder

110g pecan nuts, roughly chopped

150g chewy toffees, chopped

NUTRITION NOTES

A very tasty cake but one to save for an occasional treat as the toffee makes it extremely high in sugar. The pecans and bananas do give some benefit (nuts are high in essential fats, protein and magnesium, while bananas are a good source of soluble fibre and potassium), but you would be better off eating them on their own if you're trying to be healthy.

1   Preheat the oven to 170°C/325°F/Gas 3. Line a 1kg loaf tin with greaseproof paper.

2   In a large mixing bowl, combine the bananas, eggs, butter, yoghurt and sugar.

3   Sift in the flour and baking powder and fold together. Gently mix in half of the pecans and toffees. Spoon into the prepared tin, and sprinkle the remainder of the nuts and toffee on top.

4   Bake in the preheated oven for 50–55 minutes until the cake feels springy to the touch. Allow to cool.

Variations

For a slightly lighter version you could use natural yoghurt and omit the toffees. For children under five you could omit the nuts. For more fibre you could use half wholewheat flour.

Moist lemon cake

Sent in by Priti from Lewisham.

Makes about 8 slices

Suitable for ages 1 year +

✳ **Will freeze**

Nutrition   ⬭ Fat   ⬭ Saturates   ⬬ Sugar   ⬭ Salt

110g butter

175g caster sugar

175g self-raising flour

1 level tsp baking powder

2 large eggs

finely grated rind of 1 large or 2
  small lemons

60ml milk

DRIZZLING SAUCE

3 tbsp granulated sugar

juice of the lemons

NUTRITION NOTES

While cakes made with sugar, white
flour and butter are never going to be
exactly saintly, at least this one
contains some vitamin C (from the
lemons) and protein and
vitamins/minerals in the eggs and milk.

1   Preheat the oven to 180°C/350°F/Gas 4. Lightly grease a
    450g loaf tin.

2   Put everything except the sauce ingredients in a food
    processor and whiz until really smooth (the mixture is
    quite runny). Pour into the prepared loaf tin and bake in the
    preheated oven for 40–50 minutes.

3   Meanwhile, dissolve the sugar for the sauce in the lemon
    juice.

4   Test that the cake is done by inserting a metal skewer into
    the centre. If it comes out clean it's OK.

5   Place the cake, still in its tin, on a cooling rack and prick all
    over with a skewer. Spoon over all the sugar/lemon liquid
    and leave the cake in the tin until quite cold.

Small Cakes and Muffins

If you buy those packs of small (and high cost!) factory-made cakes at the supermarket they are likely to contain artificial flavourings, colourings and perhaps trans fats, as well as being very high in sugar and even salt. So if you make your own, they may not be nutritionally completely above reproach – but they're getting there!

Rock cakes

Sent in by Dom from Poole.

Makes about 10 cakes

Suitable for ages 1 year +

Nutrition ⬭ Fat ⬭ Saturates ⬬ Sugar ◯ Salt

250g self-raising flour

1/2 tsp mixed spice

90g unsalted butter

90g soft brown sugar

125g raisins

1 medium egg, beaten

NUTRITION NOTES
Use half wholemeal and half white self-raising flour to make it healthier.
Unsalted butter is always a good option in cooking.

1 Preheat the oven to 200ºC/400ºF/Gas 6, and lightly grease a baking tray.

2 Tip the flour and spice into a mixing bowl and rub the butter in until it resembles breadcrumbs.

3 Add the sugar and raisins, mix, and then add the egg and combine well.

4 Form into about 10 rocky heaps with your hands (kids love this bit) and put on the tray. Bake in the preheated oven for 15 minutes. Remove and allow to cool.

Variations

You can make mini versions which are great for parties. You can use 125g choc chips instead of the raisins.

Yoghurt fairy cakes

Sent in by Melanie from Peterborough, who says: '*I made these cakes for my son's playgroup at Christmas and the kids ate the lot!*'

Makes 12 cakes

Suitable for ages 1 year +

Nutrition   ● Fat   ◌ Saturates   ● Sugar   ◌ Salt

125g sunflower spread

125g caster sugar

2 medium eggs, beaten

1 x 125g pot fruit-flavoured
 yoghurt

100g self-raising flour

ICING AND DECORATION

100g soft cream cheese

40g icing sugar

1 tbsp marmalade

hundreds and thousands

NUTRITION NOTES
These cakes are high in sugar, so best
kept for occasional use.

1 Preheat the oven to 190°C/375°F/Gas 5. Line a bun tin with
   paper cases.

2 Put the sunflower spread and caster sugar in a bowl with
   the beaten eggs, half the yoghurt, and the self-raising flour.
   Using an electric whisk, beat to a smooth batter.

3 Pour into the paper cases, and bake in the preheated oven
   for 18–20 minutes until springy to the touch. Cool on a
   wire rack.

4 For the icing, beat the cream cheese, icing sugar and
   marmalade together. Once the cakes are cool spread them
   with the icing, and sprinkle a few hundreds and thousands
   on top.

Carrot cake muffins

Sent in by Ira from South Shields, who says: *'My kids both love this. I started making it as a way of getting them to eat carrot even though they didn't eat "real" carrots. They've progressed on to the real thing now but we still make the cake from time to time.'*

Makes about 12 muffins

Suitable for ages 1 year +

❄ **Will freeze if well wrapped in foil or similar**

Nutrition ◐ Fat ◯ Saturates ● Sugar ◯ Salt

---

2 medium eggs

100g soft brown sugar

5 tbsp sunflower oil

150g grated carrot

100g self-raising flour

¹/₂ tsp ground cinnamon

100g any dried fruit/s (chopped apricots, raisins, glacé cherries)

NUTRITION NOTES

High in carotenoids, fibre and iron, this is a pretty healthy recipe as cakes go.

TIP

You can make a quick topping by beating together 225g 8% fat natural fromage frais, a little runny honey and a squeeze of lemon juice. Chill and spread over the muffins or loaf.

1. Preheat the oven to 190ºC/375ºF/Gas 5. Line a muffin pan with paper cases.

2. In a bowl, mix the eggs and sugar, then beat in the oil. Add the remaining ingredients and mix again.

3. Spoon into the muffin cases and bake in the preheated oven for 15–20 minutes until firm to the touch and golden brown. Allow to cool.

Variations

You can use the mix in a 500g loaf tin instead – cook for 5–10 minutes or so longer. You can use wholemeal self-raising flour. You can omit the dried fruit (but you will have one or two fewer muffins).

Apple, oat and sultana muffins

Sent in by Amanda from the north-west.

Makes about 12 muffins

Suitable for ages 1 year +

Nutrition ⬤ Fat   ⬤ Saturates   ⬤ Sugar   ⬤ Salt

1 medium egg, beaten

100ml sunflower oil

175ml full fat milk

125g porridge oats

1 tbsp baking powder

100g self-raising flour

75g caster sugar

$1/2$ tsp mixed spice

$1/2$ tsp ground cinnamon

150g sultanas

1 apple, peeled, cored and diced

NUTRITION NOTES

Again a healthy recipe, high only in sugar – but the oats and oil mean that the sugar is absorbed less quickly into the blood and helps avoid the sugar highs that less healthy cakes might give your children.

1   Preheat the oven to 180°C/350°F/Gas 4. Line bun tins or muffin pans with paper cases.

2   Combine the beaten egg with the sunflower oil and milk (it looks horrid at this stage but the muffins taste amazing when cooked!)

3   In a large bowl mix all the remaining ingredients. Pour the egg mixture into the flour mixture but don't *over*-mix.

4   Pour into the lined bun or muffin cases and bake in the preheated oven until risen and golden, about 20 minutes. Allow to cool.

Variations

You can use chopped dessert pear instead of the apple.

Chocolate brownies

Makes 16 small squares or 12 oblongs

Suitable for ages 5 years + (or 1 year + if not using nuts)

Nutrition ●Fat ●Saturates ●Sugar ◯Salt

150g dark chocolate

115g butter

115g self-raising flour

65g caster sugar

2 medium eggs, beaten

50g shelled walnut pieces or choc
  chips

NUTRITION NOTES

As the brownies are high in fat and sugar, they are best reserved for occasional treats. However, the dark chocolate and the eggs mean that the children will be getting some iron and other minerals.

1   Preheat the oven to 180°C/350°F/Gas 4. Grease and line a 20cm square shallow baking tin with foil and lightly grease that too.

2   Break the chocolate into pieces and place in a bowl over a saucepan of barely simmering water with the butter. Make sure that the bowl doesn't touch the water. Stir occasionally until melted. Leave to cool a little.

3   Sieve the flour into a separate bowl and stir in the caster sugar. Tip the beaten eggs into the chocolate mixture and stir to combine, then tip the chocolate mix into the flour along with the nuts or choc chips and mix well to combine.

4   Pour the mixture into the foil-lined tin and bake for 25 minutes, or until just firm to the touch. Leave to cool in the tin then lift out (using the foil edges, this is an easy job) and cut into 16 squares or 12 oblongs.

Variations

Omit the walnuts, or use chopped mixed nuts or other nuts of choice.

Drop scones (or mini pancakes)

Anita from Norwich says: *'These mini pancakes are fun to make and delicious to eat – really good for an after-school snack.'*

Makes about 18 scones

Suitable for ages 1 year +

Nutrition   Fat   Saturates   Sugar   Salt

110g self-raising flour

60g caster sugar

1 medium egg

150ml milk

butter

NUTRITION NOTES

These mini pancakes are a great alternative to cake (which is higher in fat) at teatime or for a snack. The egg and milk add protein.

SERVING SUGGESTIONS

Serve with melted butter or with honey or jam.

1   In a bowl, mix together the flour and sugar. Beat the egg in another bowl, add the milk, then beat again. Add the egg and milk to the flour and sugar and mix well to make a batter. If you are using an electric whisk you can just add the milk and mix all at the same time. If you are mixing by hand (with a fork), add the milk mixture slowly and make sure everything is smooth before adding the next lot of liquid. If you get any lumps just whisk until they disappear.

2   Use a large non-stick frying pan and add a knob of butter to coat the pan. When the pan is hot and the butter beginning to sizzle (but not burn) take a dsp of batter at a time and let the batter pour from the spoon on to the pan to form a little circle. Then do another beside that one and another. You should be able to fit about eight round the outside and a couple more in the middle.

3   Then go back to the first one and turn it using a fish slice. The scones take about 60 seconds each side. As they cook, put them on to a plate. Once that batch is done, add a little more butter to the pan and do the last batch.

Biscuits and Flapjacks

Biscuits and flapjacks are quite quick and very easy to make, and you will feel much less guilty popping one into your children's lunch box than if you give them commercial ones.

Easy oaty biscuits

Makes 24 biscuits

Suitable for ages 1 year +

Nutrition ● Fat ● Saturates ● Sugar ◌ Salt

100g butter

50g caster sugar

100g rolled oats

50g plain flour

NUTRITION NOTES

Oats are a good source of soluble fibre. Home-made biscuits made with butter are a great alternative to shop-bought ones which often contain hydrogenated (trans) fats.

1 Preheat the oven to 170°C/ 325°F/Gas 3, and lightly grease a baking tray.

2 Cream the butter and sugar together. Add the oats and flour and work the mixture into a dough. Knead until smooth and then roll out thinly on a floured surface.

3 Cut into biscuits with a shaped cutter and place on the greased baking trays.

4 Bake in the preheated oven for 20 minutes until golden brown. Leave to cool on the tray for about 5 minutes, then finish cooling on a wire rack.

Flapjacks

Makes 12 flapjacks

Suitable for ages 1 year +

Nutrition   ● Fat   ● Saturates   ● Sugar   ○ Salt

100g butter

50g demerara sugar

50g golden syrup

200g rolled oats

NUTRITION NOTES
While the flapjacks are high in sugar and fat, they contain plenty of oats which are high in soluble fibre.

1 Preheat the oven to 190°C/375°F/Gas 5.

2 Melt the butter in a saucepan, then add the rest of the ingredients and stir for a minute or two.

3 Spoon the mixture into a square shallow baking tin and bake in the preheated oven for 20 minutes or until golden brown.

4 When still warm in the tin, mark into 12 oblongs. When cool, remove from tin and break into the oblong pieces.

Variations
You can add chopped dried apricots or sultanas to the mix or use muesli instead of the oats (for older children only, as children under five shouldn't eat nut pieces).

Fruit and nut cookies

Makes 30 cookies

Suitable for ages 5 years +

Nutrition   ● Fat   ● Saturates   ● Sugar   ○ Salt

cooking oil spray

125g butter

150g golden caster sugar

1 medium egg

75g wholemeal flour

75g plain white flour

1/2 tsp baking powder

125g crunchy peanut butter

100g sultanas

75g chopped dried apricots

1 Preheat the oven to 190°C/375°F/Gas 5. Spray two heavy-duty non-stick baking sheets with the cooking oil spray.

2 In a mixing bowl, combine the butter, sugar, egg, flours, baking powder and peanut butter until well mixed, then stir in the sultanas and apricots.

3 Spoon 30 small spoonfuls of the mixture on to the baking sheets, and bake in the preheated oven for 15 minutes or until the cookies are turning golden brown.

4 Cool a little and then remove with a spatula to wire racks to finish cooling.

Useful addresses

Allergy UK
3 White Oak Square, London Road, Swanley,
Kent BR8 7AG
Tel: 01322 619898 • Website: www.allergyuk.org

Asthma UK
Summit House, 70 Wilson Street, London EC2A 2DB
Tel: 08457 010203 • Website: www.asthma.org.uk

British Dietetic Association
5th Floor, Charles House, 148–149 Great Charles Street,
Queensway, Birmingham B3 3HT
Tel: 0121 200 8080 • Website: www.bda.uk.com

Coeliac UK
Octagon Court, High Wycombe, Bucks HP11 2HS
Tel: 01494 437278 • Website: www.coeliac.co.uk

Department of Health
Richmond House, 79 Whitehall, London SW1A 2NS
Tel: 020 7210 4850 • Website: www.dh.gov.uk

DEFRA
Nobel House, 17 Smith Square, London SW1P 3JR
Tel: 08459 335577 • Website: www.defra.gov.uk

Diabetes UK
Macleod House, 10 Parkway, London NW1 7AA
Tel: 020 7424 1000 • Website: www.diabetes.org.uk

Eating Disorders Association
103 Prince of Wales Road, Norwich NR1 1DW
Adult helpline: 0845 634 1414 • Website: www.edauk.com

Food and Behaviour Research
The Green House, Beechwood Business Park,
Inverness IV2 3ED
Tel: 0870 756 5960 • Website: www.fabresearch.org

Food Commission
94 White Lion Street, London N1 9PF
Tel: 020 7837 2250 • Website: www.foodcomm.org.uk

Food Standards Agency
Aviation House, 125 Kingsway, London WC2B 6NH
Tel: 020 7276 8829 • Website: www.food.gov.uk

Foresight Preconception
178 Hawthorn Road, West Bognor, West Sussex PO21 2UY
Tel: 01243 868001
Website: www.foresight-preconception.org.uk

Friends of the Earth
26–28 Underwood Street, London N1 7JQ
Tel: 020 7490 1555 • Website: www.foe.co.uk

Hyperactive Children's Support Group
71 Whyke Lane, Chichester, West Sussex PO19 7PD
Tel: 01243 551313
Email: contact@hacsg.org.uk • Website: www.hacsg.org.uk

Institute of Child Health
30 Guildford Street, London WC1N 1EH
Tel: 020 7242 9789 • Website: www.ich.ucl.ac.uk

National Association for Colitis and
Crohn's Disease
4 Beaumont House, Sutton Road, St Albans, Herts
AL1 5HH
Tel: 01727 844296 • Website: www.nacc.org.uk

Obesity Resource Information Centre
ORIC16, The Courtyard, Woodlands, Bradley Stoke, Bristol
BS32 4NQ
Tel: 01454 616798 • Website: http://aso.org.uk

Soil Association
Bristol House, 40–56 Victoria Street, Bristol BS1 6BY
Tel: 0117 314 5000 • Website: www.soilassociation.org

Sustain
94 White Lion Street, London N1 9PF
Tel: 020 7837 1228 • Website: www.sustainweb.org

Vegetarian Society
Parkdale, Dunham Road, Altrincham, Cheshire WA14 4QG
Tel: 0161 925 2000 • Website: www.vegsoc.org

Index